BOOK GIRL'S GUIDE TO

Cocktails
For Book Lovers

Tessa Smith McGovern

Published by Sourcebooks, Inc.
P.O. Box 4410, Naperville, Illinois 60567-4410
(630) 961-3900
Fax: (630) 961-2168
www.sourcebooks.com

Library of Congress Cataloging-in-Publication Data

Smith McGovern, Tessa.
  Cocktails for book lovers / Tessa Smith McGovern.
    pages cm
  Includes bibliographical references and index.
  (hard cover : alk. paper) 1. Cocktails. 2. Cocktails in literature. I. Title.
  TX951.S627 2014
  641.87'4–dc23

2014011626

Printed and bound in The United States of America.

WOZ 10 9 8 7 6 5 4 3 2 1

In joyous memory of my dad, Ken Smith (aka Papa Ken), who always loved a good time and made the best champagne cocktails.

1934–2013

CONTENTS

INTRODUCTION

G rowing up in England, I was obsessed with Virginia Woolf—her luminous prose, her melancholy brilliance—and the glamorous image of the Bloomsbury set, a famous group of London intellectuals and writers in the early 1900s. After moving to the United States at the age of thirty, I was delighted to discover the Bloomsbury set had an American counterpart: the Algonquin Round Table in New York City, an equally famous group of intellectuals and writers, led by the acerbic and amusing Dorothy Parker. The elegance of these writers and their Bohemian lifestyle, mixing and mingling over literature and libations! The parties! The cocktails! The witty repartee! It all added up to the most glamorous life I could imagine.

How glorious, then, to witness a renaissance in the popularity of cocktails in our society today. Cocktails, conversation, and culture have always gone well together, and now, with this book, you can marry these delectable concoctions with delightful prose and compelling stories from fifty contemporary and classic authors. Each entry pairs an author with a cocktail recipe that's inspired by either one of their works or a popular drink from their era, as well as an excerpt, a bio, and an additional book recommendation. It's a fabulous, chic pairing that makes perfect sense.

Imagine this book is a box of chocolates—dip in and choose the most enticing author and cocktail, or start at the beginning and work your way through to the end. Have a party! Regale your book club! Cheers!

ISABEL ALLENDE

Eva Luna

I sabel Allende was born in 1942 into the cauldron of Latin American politics. Her father was the ambassador to Peru and first cousin to Chile's president, Salvador Allende. When she was three, her father disappeared and the family took refuge in Santiago, Chile. She began telling stories to calm the fears of her two younger brothers.

At twenty, she married Miguel Frias, a former classmate. Decades later, after their divorce, she likened being his wife to serving "as his geisha." While raising their two children, Allende translated Barbara Cartland's romance novels into English, until her habit of altering retrograde dialogue and demeaning characterizations of women got her fired. Later, as a TV journalist, she interviewed the poet Pablo Neruda, who told Allende her imaginative gifts would find full expression only in novel writing.

In 1973, during a military coup, the Allendes escaped to Venezuela. She continued working as a journalist for almost a decade, until her first success, *The House of the Spirits*, became a bestseller. This sealed her association with magic realism, a style that combines fantastic, dreamlike elements with realistic fiction.

Allende is now an American citizen. She lives in San Rafael, California, with her long-time partner, attorney Willie Gordon.

Allende holds to a practice unique among writers; she always begins a new novel on January 8, a tradition that stems from a letter she wrote to her dying grandfather that day in 1981.

From *Eva Luna*:
"She treated me with kindness, even a certain tenderness. She worried that I did not eat enough; she bought me a good bed; and every afternoon she invited me into the living room to listen to the serials on the radio..."

MADRINA'S BANANA RUM COCKTAIL

Madrina is Spanish for "godmother." In this novel, the protagonist, Eva Luna's *madrina*, who assumed care of the nine-year-old Eva after her mother died, was a faithful Catholic and a lover of rum.

> 1/8 cup low-fat milk
>
> 1 tbsp. light rum
>
> 1 tbsp. white crème de cacao
>
> 1 tbsp. crème de banana (or other banana liqueur)
>
> 1/2 banana
>
> Wedge of pineapple
>
> Maraschino cherry

Place all ingredients except the fruit in a shaker with ice. Shake well. Strain into a chilled glass and garnish with fruit. Serves 1.

ALSO RECOMMENDED:
Maya's Notebook. A coming-of-age story and startling novel of suspense about a remarkable teenager abandoned by her parents.

DIANA ATHILL

Somewhere Towards the End

In 1917, famed English editor Diana Athill was born into an upper-middle-class life in Norfolk, England, complete with a stately mansion and servants. But life wasn't easy: the family finances were foundering, and her parents were deeply unhappy together. In her late teens she discovered that her sister, Patience, had been conceived as a result of her mother's affair with an army officer.

At fifteen, Athill fell in love with Tony Irvine, an Oxford graduate and RAF pilot. They were engaged to be married when he left for World War II but, after two years, he wrote asking to be released from their engagement so he could marry someone else. Shortly afterward, he was killed in action. The pain of this event devastated her for the next twenty years and resulted in an aversion to being tied down; in numerous affairs she was "the other woman." In 1951, she and the Hungarian publisher André Deutsch put together the company that bore his name. As an editor, she worked closely with legendary authors such as Norman Mailer, Simone du Beauvoir, and Margaret Atwood.

Athill began writing in earnest in her early forties. She wrote *Somewhere Towards the End*, a memoir, at the age of eighty-nine. Almost a decade later and in assisted living, Athill does not count out the possibility of another memoir.

She has said, "I think the fact that I'm in my nineties and still *compos mentis*, and able to write and have a nice time, is encouraging to people. They can look at me and say, 'There is somebody who is old—which I am dreading—but there, it's not so bad.'"

From *Somewhere Towards the End*:
"...One life can contain serenity and tumult, heartbreak and happiness, coldness and warmth, grabbing and giving..."

DIVINE GREENTINI

Diana Athill's mother's last words before she died, in describing her final gardening activity of going to buy a eucalyptus tree to plant: "It was absolutely divine."

- 1½ oz. Midori
- 1½ oz. gin
- 1 maraschino cherry

Shake ingredients, except the cherry, in a shaker and pour into a martini glass. Garnish with the cherry. Serves 1.

ALSO RECOMMENDED:
Yesterday Morning. A vivid, compelling memoir of childhood and old age.

JANE AUSTEN

Pride and Prejudice

Jane Austen was born in 1775 in rural Hampshire, England. Her father was a clergyman, and her family was comfortable, but not wealthy. She had only a few years of formal schooling (typical for girls then), but it was a lively, literate household. She adored her elder sister (her mother reportedly said that if Cassandra were going to have her head cut off, Jane would too), and loved balls and parties.

She was a precocious writer; at fourteen she completed a novel, *Love and Friendship*, a sophisticated satire of popular romantic fiction; in her version, clichés like fainting spells and wild coincidences are the stuff of ridicule.

At seventeen, she began writing her major works, beginning with *Lady Susan* and *Sense and Sensibility*, then, in her early twenties, the first draft of what would become *Pride and Prejudice*, her best-known work. Her first four books were published anonymously, the last two posthumously: *Emma*, and the melancholy *Persuasion*.

At twenty-one, she fell in love with Tom Lefroy, a young man whose family disapproved of the match. Marriage was impractical since neither had money, and he was sent away. In 1802, Austen received her only proposal of marriage, from an unattractive but wealthy suitor. She accepted, but the following morning withdrew her acceptance, despite the financial security the marriage would have offered. This event may have inspired some events in her novels, such as *Pride and Prejudice* and *Emma*. A keen observer with great wit, her works still resonate with readers today. She died at age forty-one.

From *Pride and Prejudice*:
"It is a truth universally acknowledged, that a single man in possession of a good fortune must be in want of a wife."

MISS AUSTEN'S DELIGHT

It's little-known that Jane Austen was a sophisticated reveler and wine drinker. One very popular drink in nineteenth century England was Madeira, a fortified wine.

- 1 oz. gin
- 1 oz. Malmsey (Madeira)
- 1 tsp. orange juice (optional)
- 2 maraschino cherries

Shake ingredients except the cherries with ice and strain into a cocktail glass. Garnish with maraschino cherries. Serves 1.

ALSO RECOMMENDED:

Mansfield Park. Dependent on the benevolence of her aristocratic relatives, young Fanny Price develops into the moral center of a family gone astray and restores the tranquility of her adoptive home.

ALAN BENNETT

The Complete Talking Heads

Alan Bennett was born in West Yorkshire, the son of a stoic Leeds butcher and a mother who suffered from periodic depression. He grew up in the 1930s, constantly being warned to be quiet and well-behaved.

Bennett planned on joining the clergy, but instead attended Oxford University on scholarship. There, he took in a lecture by the famous poet W. H. Auden, whom Bennett found to be such a bore that he was nearly turned off writing altogether. Bennett thereafter determined to write literature "with a small l."

His breakthrough came with *Beyond the Fringe*, a satiric revue he co-wrote with Peter Cooke, Dudley Moore, and Jonathan Miller. A transatlantic hit in 1960, the show brought Bennett instant fame. His best-known plays are *The Madness of George III* and *The History Boys*. *The Complete Talking Heads* is a collection of sharply humorous monologues that were filmed by the BBC and aired by PBS, as well as performed onstage.

While Bennett is regarded as a national treasure in England and has received countless honors, he has rejected his country's offer of a knighthood, not because he harbors republican sympathies, but because he didn't think he could carry it off. He said, "It would be like wearing a suit every day of your life." He lives in Camden Town with Rupert Thomas, his longtime partner.

From *The Complete Talking Heads*: "Miss Fozzard Finds Her Feet": "I don't know what's got into people at work. I come in this morning and the commissionaire with the moustache who's on the staff door says, 'Have a good day, my duck.' I said, 'You may only have one arm, Mr. Capstick, but that doesn't entitle you to pat me on the bottom.'"

SWEET SHERRY COCOA

In *The Complete Talking Heads*, Miss Fozzard, often comically ignorant of people's real intentions, accepts a glass of sweet sherry from Mr. Dunderdale, her new chiropodist, thinking it's just a kind gesture.

  6 oz. whole milk

  1/8 cup hot cocoa mix

  1 tbsp. sweet sherry

  Whipped cream (optional)

  Peppermint stick (optional)

Warm the milk in a saucepan, then whisk in cocoa mix and sherry. Pour into a mug and top with whipped cream and a peppermint stick, if desired. Serves 1.

ALSO RECOMMENDED:
Smut: Two Unseemly Stories. Alan Bennett, author of *The History Boys*, as you've never read him. Two tender, surprising novellas dealing with sexuality.

ANNE BRONTË

Agnes Grey

The youngest of the famed Brontë sisters, and usually considered the meekest and least important, Anne, born in 1820, was in fact quite advanced for her time. And, despite her subdued demeanor, she is the only sister who had a sustained career (as a governess). In addition, she wrote a novel, *The Tenant of Wildfell Hall* which was so disturbing and controversial that her sister Charlotte refused to have it republished after Anne's death.

Like her sisters Emily and Charlotte, Anne Brontë grew up impoverished in Yorkshire. At nineteen, Anne became a governess for some impossibly unruly children, and was dismissed when she couldn't control them. (She made good use of the episode in her first novel, *Agnes Grey*.) She then found a much more congenial post with a wealthy family near the city of York and her charges became her lifelong friends.

Eventually, however, homesickness brought her back to her family's house, where she started writing in earnest. Her bestselling second novel, *The Tenant of Wildfell Hall*, is about a debauched alcoholic and his strong-willed wife. In Victorian England, the heroine's bid for independence was not only scandalous, but illegal.

Sadly, Anne was unable to write much more. It is said that her grief at Emily's death may have hastened her own. She succumbed to tuberculosis at age twenty-nine.

From *Agnes Grey*:
"...when I got free of the town, when my foot was on the sands and my face toward the bright, broad bay...no language can describe the effect of the deep, clear azure of the sky and ocean, the bright morning sunshine on the semi-circular barrier of craggy cliffs surmounted by green swelling hills, and on the smooth, wide sands, and the low rocks out at sea..."

BRANDY EGGNOG

In *Agnes Grey*, Sir Thomas Ashby, husband of Lady Ashby, formerly Miss Murray, drinks "bottles of wine and glasses of brandy."

1¼ oz. milk

1 oz. brandy

1/2 oz. simple syrup*

1 egg yolk

Ground cinnamon

*Simple syrup is equal parts sugar and water. Boil until sugar dissolves and allow to cool.

Pour all ingredients except ground cinnamon into a cocktail shaker with ice cubes. Shake well. Strain into a stemmed cocktail glass. Dust cinnamon on top and serve. Serves 1.

ALSO RECOMMENDED:
The Tenant of Wildfell Hall. A woman makes the unconventional decision to leave her abusive husband, a book framed by Anne's belief in universal salvation (the doctrine that all sinful souls will ultimately be reconciled to God because of divine love and mercy).

CHARLOTTE BRONTË

Jane Eyre

Charlotte was the oldest surviving daughter of the three remarkable Brontë sisters, who were raised by their father in the mid-nineteenth century in a strict Church of England parsonage on the Yorkshire moors. She and her siblings had unusual and mostly solitary childhoods, centered on an imaginary kingdom they devised, for whose inhabitants they wrote obsessive, elaborate adventures.

A scheme to open a school came to nothing when no students applied, but they desperately needed an income, so Charlotte arranged for the publication of the Brontë girls' poems under the pseudonyms Currer, Ellis, and Acton Bell. Soon after, she published her first novel, *Jane Eyre*, a bestseller that brought her the then-amazing income of £500. The book, with its beloved, fiercely independent heroine and bittersweet ending, has endured as well as any English novel.

Charlotte, though devastated by the early deaths of her two sisters (Emily died in 1848, at age thirty, and Anne died in 1849, at age twenty-nine), not only wrote a second novel but made many friends among the English literati, including William Thackeray and Elizabeth Gaskell. In 1854, she married her father's curate, Arthur B. Nicholls. She wasn't in love with him, but she was scarred by her losses and greatly moved at the depth of his love for her.

Less than a year later, pregnant with her first child, she contracted pneumonia and died just before her thirty-ninth birthday.

From *Jane Eyre*:
"Prejudices, it is well known, are most difficult to eradicate from the heart whose soil has never been loosened or fertilized by education: they grow there, firm as weeds among stones."

NEGUS (MULLED WINE)

In Brontë's famed novel, Jane Eyre arrives at Thornfield, home of the absent Mr. Rochester, to become governess to Adela Varens. Mrs. Fairfax, the housekeeper, offers her a little hot negus, a mulled wine popular in Victorian times.

1 pint port wine	1 orange wheel
1 quart water	Cinnamon stick
1/4 lb. sugar	Star anise
Juice of one lemon	Grated nutmeg

Put the wine into a pitcher. In a saucepan, bring water to a boil. Add the sugar, lemon juice, and grated nutmeg. Pour the boiling water into the jug, stir, and add orange wheel, cinnamon stick and star anise. Serves 9–10.

ALSO RECOMMENDED:
Villette. At the height of her artistic power, Charlotte Brontë drew on her loneliness after the death of her three siblings to write *Villette*, her most accomplished and deeply felt work.

EMILY BRONTË

Wuthering Heights

The most tormented, most peculiar, and probably the most gifted of the Brontë sisters, Emily Brontë also grew up in the mid-nineteenth century on the Yorkshire moors. As mentioned, she invented imaginary kingdoms with her siblings and filled notebooks with the deeds of their inhabitants, working on that project until her death.

Theirs was not a happy household. Their father was a solitary, depressed eccentric. Their brother Branwell, addicted to both opium and alcohol, was given to violent rages and threats. Emily was a natural recluse. According to her sister Charlotte, "except to go to church or take a walk on the hills, she rarely crossed the threshold of home," and she was said to prefer the company of her dog, Keeper, to the company of humans. The dog shared her views—he was vicious with everyone but Emily.

Emily's health was always precarious. She nursed her brother through tuberculosis, and then caught cold at his funeral. She died a month later, also of tuberculosis, having refused all medical help. Her only novel, *Wuthering Heights*, is a stunning achievement, full of violence, passion, and uncontrolled emotion. Its strange atmosphere, heightened language, and tortured characters destroyed by love would seem to be alien to a shy, retiring parson's daughter.

From *Wuthering Heights*:
"The same conviction had stricken him as me, from the instant he beheld her, that there was no prospect of ultimate recovery there—she was fated, sure to die. 'O Cathy! Oh, my life! How can I bear it?' was the first sentence he uttered, in a tone that did not seek to disguise his despair."

HEATHCLIFF'S CRUSH

In the beginning of *Wuthering Heights*, Mr. Lockwood, the story's narrator and Heathcliff's tenant at nearby Thrushcross Grange, arrives at Wuthering Heights. Heathcliff commands Joseph to bring up some wine, and insists that Lockwood join him in a drink.

1 oz. Madeira wine	Splash of orange juice
1 oz. berry vodka	Raspberries and blueberries
2 oz. Elderflower Presse	for garnish
Ice	

Mix Madeira, vodka, and Elderflower Presse in a glass with ice. Add a float of orange juice, and raspberries and blueberries for garnish. Serves 1.

ALSO RECOMMENDED:
Poems by Currer, Ellis, and Acton Bell. This book is a reproduction of the original 1846 publication, maintaining the same format as the original.

WILLA CATHER

Cather Novels & Stories 1905–1918

Willa Cather was born in 1873 and grew up in Red Cloud, Nebraska, a place that would serve as background for many of her works. In her teens, she determined that she would become a surgeon, then considered an impossible profession for women. Accordingly, she did her best to take on a male identity: chopped off her hair, signed herself "William," dressed in men's clothing, learned Latin, dissected animals, and got a job delivering mail on horseback—behavior that scandalized the town.

In college, she began to write, and after college she moved to Pittsburgh and wrote for a newspaper. In 1906, Cather moved to New York, working for *McClure's*, a prominent muckraking literary magazine. She was conservative in her politics, but unafraid to be outrageous in her appearance and her way of life. Another journalist, Edith Lewis, became her lifelong companion—first in an apartment in Greenwich Village and then in a summer house on a secluded island off the Canadian coast. Cather never used overtly gay themes in her books, and she burned her personal papers and letters, but she often wrote about female characters from a male point of view. It's assumed she was a lesbian.

Beginning with *O Pioneers!* many of her books included fictionalized versions of people she once knew. It was Cather's gift to transform the stories of her childhood into art, both universal and particular, that immortalizes the landscape, history, and immigrant experience of America.

From *Cather Novels & Stories 1905–1918*:
"...Mrs. Kronborg was sitting up in bed darning stockings...She was a woman whom Dr. Archie respected; active, practical, unruffled; good-humored, but determined. Exactly the sort of woman to take care of a flighty preacher."

PETER'S WHISKEY COCKTAIL

In her poignant short story, "Peter," included in *Friends of Childhood* (and originally published in 1892 in *The Mahogany Tree*, a weekly literary magazine), Cather wrote that Peter would pawn his hat or coat to buy whiskey.

| 1½ oz. bourbon, rye, or
| blended whiskey
| Club soda
| Ginger ale

Fill a highball glass with ice and add bourbon. Fill with equal parts club soda and ginger ale. Serves 1.

ALSO RECOMMENDED:
The Selected Letters of Willa Cather. In her will, Cather instructed that her private letters should never be published, but the foundations that now own them decided to share them with the public (thankfully).

KATE CHOPIN

The Awakening

Kate O'Flaherty Chopin, born in 1850, grew up in St. Louis with four generations of women, including her French Creole great-grandmother. But her fiction, which she began writing in her late thirties, was inspired by New Orleans, where she moved at nineteen when she married Oscar Chopin, a cotton broker.

Extremely unconventional for her time, Chopin smoked, drank, and never tried to hide her intelligence. When Oscar died of malaria, she was left with six children and little money. She ran Oscar's business and had an affair with a married plantation owner before finally returning to St. Louis to live with her mother.

Most of her stories are penetrating studies of characters in her colorful multiracial world; her novel *The Awakening* is an unsentimental look at a complex woman struggling with the constraints of marriage and the question of sexuality, which the book examines frankly but ambiguously: the heroine has an affair with another man, but adultery doesn't bring happiness. In the words of one scandalized reviewer, "We are well satisfied when she drowns herself."

Disheartened by the novel's hostile reception, she never published another book. Visiting the famous St. Louis World's Fair on a hot day in 1904, she developed a debilitating headache, went home to bed, and died of a brain hemorrhage two days later.

Chopin was a groundbreaking American writer whose honest, poetically written works provided insight into women and their often thwarted needs for independence, respect, and fulfilling sex lives.

From *Complete Novels and Stories*:
"The trouble is," sighed the Doctor, grasping her meaning intuitively, "that youth is given up to illusions. It seems to be a provision of Nature; a decoy to secure mothers for the race."

ANGOSTURA TODDY

In *The Awakening*, Robert offers Madame Ratignolle a toddy with a drop of Angostura to give her energy.

- **2 oz. whiskey**
- **2 dashes Angostura bitters**
- **3 oz. boiling water**
- **2 cinnamon sticks (optional)**
- **Grated nutmeg (optional)**
- **Lemon slices (optional)**

Pour whiskey and bitters into a glass. Add boiling water. Optional: garnish with lemon slice, cinnamon stick, or grated nutmeg. Serves 1.

ALSO RECOMMENDED:
The Story of an Hour. This story explores the time that elapsed between the moments when Louise Mallard heard that her husband was dead, and then discovered that he was alive after all.

COLETTE

Chéri

Sidonie-Gabrielle Colette, author of nearly eighty volumes of fiction, memoirs, journalism, and drama, was born in 1873 to a mother who loved books and nature, but could also be dominating. At twenty, Colette married a much older, established writer. The legend that he locked her in a room until she finished a novel is probably not true, but he did encourage her to write.

Her first efforts, four slightly erotic novels about a girl named Claudine, introduced the kind of character Colette would write about for the rest of her life: a smart, sexy woman with a great appetite for life. Colette also acted in music halls, notorious for exploits like baring one breast, miming sexual intercourse, and kissing another woman onstage (which nearly caused a riot; the police were called). Her novel *La Vagabonde* (1910) is about an actress who values her independence so much she rejects marriage to the man she loves. Colette, however, was married three times; her final husband was seventeen years her junior.

She had one daughter, but didn't want a child and was not a good parent. She was also an unorthodox stepmother; her controversial 1920 novel, *Chéri*, about the romance between a predatory older woman and a frivolous young man, was a groundbreaking look at reversed gender roles, supposedly inspired by her stepson.

In her later years Colette was very overweight—food was one of her great loves. She once said, famously, "If I can't have too many truffles, I'll do without truffles."

From *Chéri*:
"While April, green and cold, a-blossom with pawlonias, tulips, heaps of hyacinths, and clusters of laburnum, made Paris fragrant, Chéri buried himself, alone, in austere shadows."

CLASSIC MULLED WINE

Colette called herself "a worthy disciple of wine" who quaffed "my glass of mulled wine, aromatic, with cinnamon and lemon."

- 1 bottle red wine (Cabernet Sauvignon or Merlot)
- 1/4 cup brandy
- 8–10 cloves
- 1/3 cup honey or sugar
- 1 tsp. fresh or 2 tsp. ground ginger
- 3 cinnamon sticks (optional)
- Lemon wheel (optional)
- One peeled and sliced orange (use peel in the pot)

Combine all ingredients in a large pot. Warm on low to medium heat, avoid boiling, and stir occasionally. When well-blended, ladle into mugs, leaving the seasonings in the pot. Garnish as desired. Serves 4–6.

ALSO RECOMMENDED:
The Vagabond. A vivid portrait of Parisian music hall life, drawn from her personal experiences.

JUNOT DÍAZ

This Is How You Lose Her

Junot Díaz was born in 1968 in the Dominican Republic but grew up in Parlin, New Jersey, a small town whose best-known landmark was its strip club. The town's movie theater became his refuge, providing vital knowledge of the world beyond Parlin and nurturing his love of narrative. At fifteen, Díaz dreamed of being a history professor.

His parents' marital discord burdened Díaz and his four siblings, and the theme of absent fathers is prevalent in his work. When he was a teen, a librarian gave him an illustrated version of the Sherlock Holmes story *The Sign of Four*. In Holmes, whose acute powers of observation enabled him to make sense of the world, Díaz saw someone he wanted to emulate.

Finding his own life experience absent from literature, Díaz began writing stories. He found an agent and had an acclaimed short story collection, *Drown*, published in 1996. Ten years would pass before his next book. That decade entailed an epic struggle with creative frustration and self-doubt that led Díaz at one point to cancel his plans of being a writer and pursue academia instead. Somehow he came out on the other side with the book he wanted, *The Brief Wondrous Life of Oscar Wao*, which was awarded the 2008 Pulitzer Prize in fiction.

Díaz lives in New York and Cambridge, Massachusetts, where he teaches at MIT and edits the *Boston Review*.

From *This Is How You Lose Her*:
"Let me confess: I love Santo Domingo. I love coming home to the guys in blazers trying to push little cups of Brugal into my hands. Love the plane landing, everybody clapping when the wheels kiss the runway..."

PAPI'S RUM PUNCH

In *This Is How You Lose Her*, Yunior's father ("Papi") drinks Bermúdez rum with his friend Miguel.

- 8 oz. light rum
- 8 oz. aged rum
- 8 oz. fresh orange juice
- 8 oz. mango nectar or juice
- 4 oz. pineapple juice
- Ice
- 8 lemon wheels

In a pitcher, combine all ingredients except the lemon wheels and refrigerate until chilled, about 2 hours. Stir well and serve over ice in punch glasses. Garnish each drink with a lemon wheel. Serves 6–8.

ALSO RECOMMENDED:
The Brief Wondrous Life of Oscar Wao. The eye-opening story of an overweight ghetto nerd from the Dominican Republic who dreams of finding love.

CHARLES DICKENS

David Copperfield

Charles Dickens, born in 1812 in Portsmouth, England, was the second of eight children. His early years seem to have been idyllic. Then, in 1824, Dickens's father was forced into a London debtors' prison, and Dickens's mother and the youngest children joined him there, as was the practice at the time.

Charles, then twelve, was sent to board with an impoverished family friend and forced to work ten-hour days pasting labels on pots of boot blacking. After a few months, a small inheritance freed the family, but Dickens's mother did not immediately bring him home. He said, "I never afterwards forgot, I never shall forget, I never can forget, that my mother was warm for my being sent back." In his favorite, most autobiographical novel, *David Copperfield*, he wrote: "I had no advice, no counsel, no encouragement, no consolation, no assistance, no support, of any kind, from anyone...!"

He went back to school, worked briefly in a law office, then became a journalist. In 1836 he married Catherine Hogarth and together they had ten children. As well as a huge list of novels, he published an autobiographical fragment, edited weekly periodicals, and wrote travel books and plays. By 1858 he was estranged from his wife and had a relationship with the actress Ellen Ternan. He died in 1870 and is buried at Westminster Abbey in London.

From *David Copperfield*:
"You are too young to know how the world changes every day," said Mrs. Creakle, "and how the people in it pass away. But we all have to learn it, David; some of us when we are young, some of us when we are old..."

MR. MICAWBER'S HOT GIN PUNCH

Wilkins Micawber was a fictional character in Dicken's 1850 novel *David Copperfield*, based on Dickens's own father, who was extremely fond of hot gin punch.

- 3 cups gin
- 3 cups Madeira wine
- 4 cloves
- Pinch of grated nutmeg
- 1 teaspoon ground cinnamon
- 1 teaspoon brown sugar
- 6 lemon twists
- 3 big chunks of pineapple
- 4 teaspoons honey
- Juice of one lemon
- Dash of water
- Orange slices for garnish

Mix all the ingredients, except the orange slices, in a pot. Bring to a simmer for twenty minutes. Pour into a teapot, serve warm, and garnish with orange slices. Serves 6.

ALSO RECOMMENDED:
A Tale of Two Cities. A classic novel about the plight of the French peasants before and during the French Revolution, and their demoralization by the French aristocracy.

OLIVIA HOWARD DUNBAR

The Shell of Sense

Olivia Howard Dunbar, born in 1873, graduated from Smith College in Massachusetts and headed for New York City, where she had a successful newspaper career. By the time she left journalism in 1902 to concentrate on her own writing, she was an editor at the *New York World*. She didn't marry until her early forties, and she and her husband, a poet and playwright, were part of a lively circle of Greenwich Village writers that included Robert Frost.

Dunbar is best remembered for her contribution to the tradition of the ghost story. In an essay entitled "The Decay of the Ghost in Fiction," she pointed out that "ever since literature began... what we call 'the supernatural' has been the staple material of the tellers of tales" and added a plea for its renaissance.

Ghosts and the supernatural played a large role in her own work. Her short story "The Dream Baby," about a lesbian couple who desperately want a child, was far ahead of its time in terms of its social attitudes. "The Shell of Sense" is told from the point of view of a dead woman who watches as her widowed husband falls in love again. "The Long Chamber" is both a love story and a story of psychological suspense about a woman who has supported her husband's career at the expense of her own. The story was probably an outgrowth of Dunbar's involvement with women's rights, especially the suffragist cause.

From *The Shell of Sense*:
"To me, watching, listening, hovering. There came a dreadful purpose and a dreadful courage. Suppose, for one moment, Theresa should not only feel, but see me—would she dare to tell him then?"

CORPSE REVIVER

Olivia Howard Dunbar was an important contributor to the tradition of the ghost story in the early twentieth century, so it seems only fitting to offer this cocktail recipe as a tribute to her wonderfully macabre work.

- 1 oz. gin
- 1 oz. Lillet Blanc
- 1 oz. fresh squeezed lime juice
- 1 oz. orange liqueur (e.g. Cointreau)
- Lemon wheel for garnish

Pour all ingredients except lemon wheel into a cocktail shaker with ice. Stir well. Strain into a chilled cocktail glass. Garnish with the lemon wheel. Serves 1.

WILLIAM FAULKNER

As I Lay Dying

Named for his great-grandfather, a Civil War general, William Faulkner was born in 1897 and grew up hearing beguiling tales of the Old South told by his nanny, a former slave known as Mammy Callie.

His father was a heavy drinker who demanded complete obedience. Billy, as he was known, was an average student and a poor athlete; the back brace his mother forced him to wear for two years to correct his poor posture elicited mockery from his peers. To compensate for his lack of popularity, he became a gifted teller of yarns and a serious reader, who revered the Old Testament, *Don Quixote*, and the writings of Balzac.

His first writings were poems, and his love of poetry, nurtured by a friend, inspired Faulkner to drop out of high school in eleventh grade. He took a job at a bank owned by a relative, and, while there, discovered whiskey.

Faulkner served in the Canadian Air Force during the First World War, briefly attended college, and took jobs as a newspaper writer and bookstore employee. In 1929 he wrote his masterpiece, *The Sound and the Fury*. That year he married Estelle Oldham after she divorced her first husband.

The novels he wrote in the next twelve years sealed his reputation as a giant of twentieth-century literature. He won his first Pulitzer Prize in 1949 and spent his later years living like the old Southern aristocrat he'd dreamed of being—financed by lucrative Hollywood screen-writing jobs, including *The Big Sleep*—and basking in the glow of worldwide adulation.

From *As I Lay Dying*:
"So I saved out the eggs and baked yesterday. The cakes turned out right well. We depend a lot on our chickens. They are good layers, what few we have left after the possums and such."

MINT JULEP

William Faulkner was a notorious drinker and one of his favorite drinks was the Mint Julep.

- 4–6 fresh mint sprigs
- 2½ oz. bourbon whiskey
- 1 tsp. powdered sugar
- 2 tsp. water
- Crushed ice

Muddle mint leaves, powdered sugar, and water in a Collins glass. Fill the glass with crushed ice and add bourbon. Top with more ice and garnish with a mint sprig. Serve with a straw. Serves 1.

ALSO RECOMMENDED:
The Unvanquished. One of Faulkner's short novels, set in Mississippi during the Civil War and Reconstruction. The Sartoris family, with their code of personal responsibility and courage, stands for the best of the Old South's traditions.

F. SCOTT FITZGERALD

The Great Gatsby

Born in 1896 in Saint Paul, Minnesota, to an upper-class Catholic family, F. Scott Fitzgerald attended the prestigious Catholic institution, the Newman School, in Hackensack, New Jersey.

At Princeton University, Scott devoted himself to humor and music writing, and let his studies wither. Without finishing, he joined the army in 1917 and quickly wrote a novel, in case he was killed in action before he had proven himself a writer.

As a soldier stationed in Alabama, he fell for eighteen-year-old Zelda Sayre. With his book's publication seemingly imminent, she agreed to marry him, but it was rejected and she broke off their engagement. In 1919, he rewrote the novel. Published as *This Side of Paradise* in 1920, it made him famous. Scott and Zelda married the following week.

The couple returned to Saint Paul, had a daughter, then bought a house in Great Neck, Long Island. Fitzgerald's play, *The Vegetable*, failed, money was tight and tensions escalated, fueled by prodigious drinking.

In 1924, seeking solace in Paris, he wrote *The Great Gatsby*, which sold modestly. In 1930, Zelda was hospitalized for the first of several breakdowns. He would later incorporate portions of her diaries into sections of his novel, *Tender Is the Night*, set in a sanitarium. Fitzgerald struggled with poor health, alcoholism, and financial woes. At forty-four, halfway through a novel, he died of a heart attack, believing himself a failed writer.

From *The Great Gatsby*:

"...girls were swooning backward playfully into men's arms...but no one swooned backward on Gatsby, and no French bob touched Gatsby's shoulder, and no singing quartets were formed with Gatsby's head for one link."

GIN RICKEY

In *The Great Gatsby*, Daisy and Gatsby take "long, greedy swallows" of their Gin Rickeys.

1½ oz. gin

Juice of half a lime

Carbonated water

Lime wheels, quartered

Pour lime juice and gin into an old-fashioned glass over ice cubes. Fill with carbonated water and stir. Add the lime. Serves 1.

ALSO RECOMMENDED:
Tender Is the Night. The tragic romance and ruination of a young psychiatrist who adores his former-patient-turned-wife. Closely modeled on real life, Fitzgerald described this book as his "confession of faith."

ELIZABETH GASKELL

Mary Barton

Elizabeth Stevenson Gaskell was born in 1810. Although her mother died young and she was rejected by her father, Gaskell nonetheless had a happy childhood, living with relatives in a town that later became the inspiration for her book of stories, *Cranford & Other Stories*. She had a passion for reading and writing, and eventually was sent to boarding school.

The early years of her marriage to a Unitarian minister were marred by miscarriages and stillbirths. They successfully raised four daughters, but the death of a baby son sent Elizabeth into a deep depression. To distract her, her husband suggested she write a novel. *Mary Barton* was published in 1848, anonymously, but it wasn't long before her identity was unmasked.

Like her contemporary, Charles Dickens, many of Gaskell's works contrast the lives of rich and poor, and her depiction of poverty was honest and compassionate. She often showed the effects of the Industrial Revolution on ordinary workers whose jobs were lost to the greed of their employers.

Gaskell was great friends with both Dickens and Charlotte Brontë, and wrote the celebrated biography, *The Life of Charlotte Brontë*. Her final novel, *Wives and Daughters*, was unfinished when she died. Her death came at a tea party when, in the midst of telling a funny story, she suddenly slumped in her chair, collapsing from a heart attack at fifty-five.

From *Mary Barton*:
"Remember, too, that though it may take much suffering to kill the able-bodied and effective members of society, it does *not* take much to reduce them to worn, listless, diseased creatures, who thenceforward crawl through life with moody hearts and pain-stricken bodies."

SMUGGLER'S RESPITE

Mary Barton, after fainting, is resuscitated by a kindly boatman who pours smuggled "Golden Wasser" into her mouth. Goldschlager is a close cousin, but tastes much better!

- **4 oz. hot coffee**
- **1/4 oz. triple sec**
- **1/4 oz. amaretto**
- **1/4 oz. Irish Cream**
- **1/4 oz. hazelnut liqueur**
- **Dash of cinnamon schnapps (Goldschlager)**
- **Whipped cream (optional)**
- **Chocolate powder (optional)**

Mix everything but the coffee and cinnamon schnapps in an Irish coffee glass. Stir in coffee and schnapps. Optional: garnish with whipped cream and chocolate powder. Serves 1.

ALSO RECOMMENDED:
Cranford & Other Stories. Charming and humorous, *Cranford* was first published in *Household Words*, a weekly magazine started by Charles Dickens in 1850.

CHARLOTTE PERKINS GILMAN

The Yellow Wall-Paper

Born in Hartford, Connecticut, in 1860, Gilman had an impoverished, strict, lonely upbringing, forbidden by her abandoned, embittered mother to read fiction or make friends with other children. Determined to educate herself, Gilman profited from the local library and from the influence of her three accomplished aunts: Harriet Beecher Stowe (who wrote *Uncle Tom's Cabin*) and the well-known suffragists and feminist advocates, Catharine and Isabella Beecher.

Gilman married an artist, Charles Walter Stetson, and gave birth to a daughter. She then suffered from postpartum depression, considered at the time a "brain disease" or "hysteria." A famous "nerve specialist" prescribed bed rest, electroshock, huge meals, and no reading, writing, or "intellectual life." The regimen brought her to "the borderline of utter mental ruin." She ended her unhappy marriage and began writing, saved by "work, in which is joy and growth and service, without which one is a pauper and a parasite."

Besides poetry and fiction, Gilman wrote feminist tracts, but is most famous for the story "The Yellow Wall-Paper," at the end of which the heroine goes mad.

At forty, she married a lawyer seven years younger who supported the causes she believed in. After he died, Gilman, diagnosed with breast cancer, committed suicide.

From *The Yellow Wall-Paper, Herland, and Selected Writings*:
"I meant to be such a help to John, such a real rest and comfort, and here I am a comparative burden already! Nobody would believe what an effort it is to do what little I am able—to dress and entertain, and order things."

YELLOW TONIC

In "The Yellow Wall-Paper," physician John insists his wife drink ale, wine, and tonics to keep her strength up, and not write, so she can recover from her "slight hysterical tendency," a diagnosis common for women suffering from depression in the 1800s.

> **6 oz. lemon vodka**
>
> **18 oz. orange juice**
>
> **4 scoops lemon sherbet**
>
> **1 cup crushed ice**
>
> **Powdered sugar**
>
> **4 slices of star fruit**

In a blender mix the vodka, orange juice, orange sherbet, and ice. Blend until smooth. Rim margarita glasses with powdered sugar. Pour into glasses and garnish with fruit. Serves 4.

ALSO RECOMMENDED:
Herland. Delightfully humorous account of three male explorers who stumble upon an all-female society in which women need men for nothing (including reproduction).

GAIL GODWIN

Evenings at Five

Gail Godwin, born in 1937, grew up in the mountains of Asheville, North Carolina, where she went to live with her mother and her grandmother, a recent widow, after Godwin's parents divorced. Her father reappeared at her high school graduation, and they reconciled. A few years later, he committed suicide.

The first story she wrote was about a henpecked husband. Inspired by the sight of her mother writing (and being paid for) newspaper articles and romance stories, she was determined to write fiction but knew that she had to be practical, so she majored in journalism.

After graduation from the University of North Carolina, she worked as a reporter for a Miami newspaper, then at the United States Travel Service at the U.S. Embassy in London, returning home after six years. She attended the University of Iowa, earning first her MA from the Iowa Writers' Workshop and then a PhD in English literature.

In 1971, Godwin published her first novel and met the composer Robert Starer. Their collaboration on an opera led to a partnership and romance that lasted until his death in 2001. An avid painter, Godwin has said that she learns about her characters by painting them.

At a writers' conference in 2012, Godwin said: "What is my emotional attitude?...[I]t's something about wanting to escape from whatever confines I'm in, and at the same time... realizing the precious gifts of the shadows to be found in those confines." Her most recent novel is *Flora*.

From *Evenings at Five*:
"Five o'clock sharp...the grinding of the ice, a growling, workmanlike sound, a lot like Rudy's own sound, compliments of the GE model Rudy had picked out fourteen years ago when they built this house... He built Christina's drink with loving precision, 'eet is cocktail time.'"

FIVE O'CLOCK SHARP

In *Evenings at Five*, every night until he died, Rudy lovingly built Christina a gin and tonic.

2 oz. gin

3/4 oz. fresh-squeezed lemon juice

1/2 oz. maraschino liqueur

Splash of tonic water

Wedge of lime

Combine all ingredients except lime wedge in a cocktail shaker with ice. Shake and strain into a cocktail glass over ice. Garnish with lime. Serves 1.

ALSO RECOMMENDED:

Violet Clay. In this coming-of-age novel, Violet Clay arrives in New York City from Charleston to take the art world by storm. But nine years, many affairs, and thousands of drinks later, it still hasn't happened.

JANE GREEN

Another Piece of My Heart

Every writer has a rejection story to tell and Jane Green, born in 1968, is no exception: an agent termed her debut novel "frankly, unpublishable"—but rather unusually, that is her *only* rejection. A week later, a bidding war broke out over the book, and she has continued to nest comfortably atop bestseller lists on two continents ever since the release of *Straight Talking* in 1996.

Working as a journalist in the UK, Green was inspired by a friend who had written a book and landed a publishing deal. The lightbulb moment came when she considered Nick Hornby's *High Fidelity* and wondered how it would sound if told by a female protagonist.

Within a year she had written *Straight Talking*, had it published, and watched it become a sensation. It quickly established her at the forefront of the chick-lit genre. Since then, her characters have matured and her fiction has evolved to reflect the issues of the women Green sees around her. Regarding her astonishing success, Green says her greatest gift is self-discipline.

She has always loved old London houses, the kind she grew up in, with their long driveways and cozy drawing rooms. The pillows, pillboxes and other items peculiar to old London houses seemed to suggest hidden stories from the past.

Green now lives in Connecticut with her second husband and their combined family of six children.

From *Another Piece of My Heart*:
"Andi knows she shouldn't open their door, shouldn't check up, but she is being a mother, she tells herself. This is what mothers do. A stepmother may not have the same rights, but she is trying...How she wishes she had children of her own."

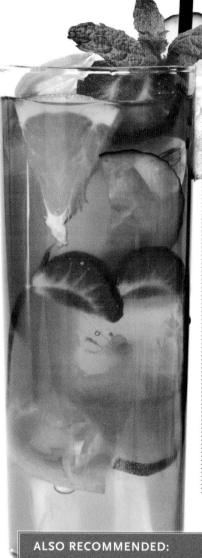

PIMM'S NO. 1 CLASSIC*
Jane Green, a modern classic English author, makes this classic cocktail in our author interview on BookGirlTV.

| 1 oz. Pimm's No. 1
| 3 oz. chilled lemon/lime soda
| 2 cucumber slices
| 2 orange slices
| 2 lemon slices
| Sliced strawberries
| 2 mint sprigs

Pour Pimm's No. 1 and lemon/lime soda over ice cubes into a tall glass. Add fruit and mint and stir. Serves 1.

*Watch the BookGirlTV video interview with Jane Green.

ALSO RECOMMENDED:
Family Pictures. Two women on opposite coasts, both mothers, both feeling unexpectedly empty, discover a shocking secret that connects them to each other and threatens to ruin their lives.

LORRAINE HANSBERRY

To Be Young, Gifted and Black

Lorraine Hansberry was born into the American civil rights struggle in 1930. Her parents, a real estate broker and a schoolteacher, challenged Chicago's restrictive housing covenants by moving into an all-white neighborhood because they believed that changing an unjust system demanded engagement with the other side. When they moved into an apartment in South Chicago where African Americans were prohibited from living, the Hansberrys fought eviction and became the center of a legal dispute that reached the Supreme Court in 1940.

Hansberry left the University of Wisconsin before graduating. She moved to New York City and wrote for *Freedom*, a magazine overseen by Paul Robeson. In 1952, when Robeson was denied a passport to attend a peace summit in Uruguay, Hansberry attended in his stead.

One year later, while protesting segregation in professional sports, Hansberry met Robert Nemiroff, a Jewish music publisher/songwriter active in social causes. Later that year, on the night before they were married, they demonstrated in support of the Rosenbergs, who were subsequently executed for espionage. Two years later, in 1957, *A Raisin in the Sun*, her signature work, debuted on Broadway, a first for a female African American playwright.

Hansberry came to embrace her identity as a lesbian during her marriage. She and Nemiroff divorced in 1964 but remained in close collaboration. Hansberry died in 1965. She was 34.

From *To Be Young, Gifted And Black: Lorraine Hansberry in Her Own Words*:
"The things he taught me were great things: that all racism was rotten, white or black, that *everything* is political; that people tend to be indescribably beautiful and uproariously funny."

MAPLE WHISKEY & CRANBERRY

In the essay "The Human Race Concerns Me," Hansberry writes: "Would like to be with a company of friends...But I am alone. Spice, scotch and me..."

> **2 oz. maple flavored whiskey**
>
> **1/2 oz. club soda**
>
> **2 dashes cranberry bitters**
>
> **Maraschino cherry (optional)**

Pour whiskey and bitters into a cocktail glass. Stir and top off with club soda. Add cherry for garnish. Serves 1.

ALSO RECOMMENDED:
A Raisin in the Sun. A groundbreaking play set on Chicago's South Side about the hopes and dreams of the Younger family and the tensions and prejudice they face.

ERNEST HEMINGWAY

The Old Man and the Sea

Ernest Hemingway was born in 1899 and grew up in Illinois, the son of a physician father and a musician mother. His father later committed suicide.

An accomplished athlete and writer for the school newspaper, Hemingway left early for a job in journalism. It was as a cub reporter for the *Kansas City Star* that he learned to write lean prose and avoid adjectives, habits that would later inform his literary work.

At eighteen, he drove an ambulance in Italy during World War I and was seriously wounded in action. During his recuperation, he fell in love with a nurse whose rejection hurt him deeply.

Once recovered, he took a job at the *Toronto Star* before moving to Chicago, where he met Hadley Richardson, the first of his four wives. They married in 1921 and moved to Paris. There, as a foreign correspondent, he became friends with Gertrude Stein. In 1923, his son was born, and Hemingway traveled to Pamplona, Spain, and witnessed bullfighting for the first time. Return trips inspired his masterpiece *The Sun Also Rises*, written in eight weeks and published in 1926.

For inventing a new minimalist literary vernacular (short, rhythmic sentences with no adjectives), Hemingway was lauded; for his exploits as an adventurer and soldier, he was viewed as a paragon of (now old-fashioned) machismo. In the end, his body wracked by injuries from surviving multiple plane crashes, paranoid and unable to write, he shot himself in Ketchum, Idaho.

From *The Old Man and the Sea*:
"He was an old man who fished alone in a skiff in the Gulf Stream and he had gone eighty-four days now without taking a fish... Everything about him was old except his eyes and they were the same color as the sea and were cheerful and undefeated."

MOJITO

Hemingway wrote extensively in his fiction about many different drinks, including the daiquiris and mojitos he consumed in great quantity in Cuba, where he lived from the 1930s until 1960.

- 1¼ oz. rum
- 12 mint leaves
- Crushed ice
- 1 tbsp. sugar
- 1/2 oz. lime juice
- 2 oz. soda
- Lime wedges

Place mint leaves in bottom of glass. Add sugar and muddle. Then add white rum (can be spiced rum too), lime juice, crushed ice, and soda water. Garnish with limes and mint leaves. Serves 1.

ALSO RECOMMENDED:
The Complete Short Stories of Ernest Hemingway. Includes beloved classics such as "The Snows of Kilimanjaro," "Hills Like White Elephants," and "A Clean, Well-Lighted Place." An invaluable treasury.

GEORGETTE HEYER

Friday's Child

Georgette Heyer, inspired by Jane Austen, is famous worldwide for her Regency romances and detective fiction.

Born in 1902 in Wimbledon, England, Heyer was the eldest of three children. In 1919, she wrote a story to entertain her brother Boris while he was ill, which her father enjoyed so much that he helped her publish it. *The Black Moth* appeared in 1921 and six years later, when Heyer was twenty-three, her father died of a heart attack. She then assumed financial responsibility for her two younger brothers. Soon after, she married and would later give birth to a son. In 1926,

she released *These Old Shades*, which appeared during the 1926 UK General Strike and, as a result, the novel received no newspaper coverage, reviews, or advertising, but still sold 190,000 copies. Thereafter, Heyer determined that publicity was not necessary for good sales and refused to promote her books.

Beginning in 1932, Heyer released one romance novel and one mystery each year. Her favorite, *Friday's Child*, written in 1944, is generally considered the best of her romances. This book outsold her mysteries and provided most of the family's earnings.

From *Friday's Child*:

"But I'm about to offer for you!" said the Viscount, with more than a touch of asperity. "I know," replied the lady. "It is useless. Say no more, my lord!" The Viscount arose from his knee, much chagrined. "I must say, Isabella, I think you might let a fellow speak!" he said crossly. "I would spare you pain, my lord." "I wish you would stop talking in that damned theatrical way!" said the Viscount. "And don't keep calling me 'my lord', as though you hadn't known me all your life!"

LORD SHERINGHAM'S RATAFIA

In *Friday's Child*, Lord Sheringham ordered ratafia for Hero Wantage, his wife-to-be (and burgundy for himself), to toast their wedding.

| 1 bottle dry white wine
| 1/4 cup peach vodka
| 1 cup of peach slices, mint,
| and rosemary
| 1/4 cup sugar
| Mint for garnish
| Orange slices for garnish

Combine all ingredients except mint sprig and orange slices in a large jar and refrigerate 2–3 days or up to a week. Strain into a pitcher and keep refrigerated. Garnish with mint sprig and orange slices. Serves 6–8.

ALSO RECOMMENDED:
Death in the Stocks. There is a murder on a moonlit night in an English village in the 1930s, and Superintendent Hannsyde must discover "whodunit." One in a series of classic English manor house mysteries, full of eccentric characters and great dialogue.

ZORA NEALE HURSTON

The Complete Stories of Zora Neale Hurston

African American writer Zora Neale Hurston, born in 1891, grew up in tiny, rural Eatonville, Florida, the first incorporated black township in the United States. Her mother always told her children to "jump at de sun," and, as Hurston said later, "We might not land on the sun, but at least we would get off the ground."

Zora was motherless by age thirteen. Her preacher father remarried a woman Zora didn't like, and Zora, bright though she was, was removed from school. She took jobs minding children and waitressing until she was hired by a white woman who, recognizing Hurston's intelligence, enrolled her in high school—at age twenty-six.

She earned degrees from Howard University and Barnard, studied anthropology at Columbia, and became an important figure in the Harlem Renaissance; her apartment became a haven for artists and writers. She traveled extensively and had two brief marriages, but spent most of her life alone.

Their Eyes Were Watching God, her vibrant depiction of the lives of blacks, was initially criticized for not trying harder to combat racism. Today, this classic novel has a wide readership and academic recognition. Hurston was poor all her life; her biggest royalty check was for $943.75. She worked in a library, substitute taught, cleaned houses, and died a recluse without even a headstone. One was supplied in 1973 by the writer Alice Walker, who recognized Hurston as a trail-blazing writer. It reads: "Zora Neale Hurston: A Genius of the South."

From *The Complete Stories:*
"Outside the tempest raged. The palms rattled dryly and the giant pines groaned and sighed in the grip of the wind. Flying leaves and pine-mast filled the air."

ORANGE BLOSSOM

Zora Neale Hurston grew up in Orange County, Florida, and blossomed into a trail-blazing writer with a sunny demeanor. Self-assured and intelligent, she rose above prejudice, saying: "How can anyone deny themselves the pleasure of my company? It's beyond me."

> 3/4 oz. gin
> 3/4 oz. sweet vermouth
> 3/4 oz. orange juice
> Orange wheel

Pour ingredients into a mixing glass with ice. Stir well. Strain into a chilled cocktail glass. Garnish with orange wheel. Serves 1.

ALSO RECOMMENDED:
I Love Myself When I Am Laughing...and Then Again When I Am Looking Mean and Impressive. A collection of all writings by Hurston, called "One of the greatest writers of our time" by Toni Morrison.

JAMES JOYCE

Ulysses

Born in Dublin in 1882, the precocious oldest child in a large, impoverished family, Joyce couldn't wait to get out of Ireland—then wrote about it all his life. He inherited his father's fine tenor voice, weakness for alcohol, and inability to support a family. Despite Joyce's literary success, he was chronically poor all his life.

Educated by the Jesuits, he earned a BA from University College in Dublin, then left for Europe, eventually taking with him Nora Barnacle, a chambermaid who became his wife: he called her his "portable Ireland." The Joyces had two children, and the family moved to Trieste, where Joyce taught English, but also spent time in Rome, Paris, and Zurich. He was a true eccentric, and had a wide circle of devoted friends who kept him afloat.

Joyce was an innovative writer whose stream-of-consciousness technique influenced much of Modernist literature. His masterpiece, *Ulysses*, was also the subject of a landmark obscenity trial. In the words of his wife, "I guess the man's a genius, but what a dirty mind he has!" (She also famously asked him, "Why don't you write books people can read?") The stories in *Dubliners* (1914) are Joyce's most accessible (and widely beloved) works. Joyce died in 1941, disappointed that *Finnegans Wake*, his last book, was generally considered incomprehensible.

Ulysses takes place in the course of one day—June 16, 1904—and that date is celebrated internationally as "Bloomsday" (after the book's hero, Leopold Bloom) with readings and pub crawls in Joyce's honor.

From *Ulysses*:
"Stately, plump Buck Mulligan came from the stairhead, bearing a bowl of lather on which a mirror and a razor lay crossed. A yellow dressing gown, ungirdled, was sustained gently behind him on the mild morning air."

RUDDY MARY

Joycean characters are known for their alcoholic overindulgence, and drinks featured in his stories include stout, whiskey, brandy, rum, porter, wine, cider, beer, and gin. The Ruddy Mary, made with gin instead of vodka (a la Bloody Mary), is often used as a pick-me-up after overindulging.

- 2 oz. gin
- 4 oz. tomato juice
- 1/2 teaspoon finely grated horseradish
- 3 dashes Worcestershire sauce
- 3 dashes Tabasco Sauce
- 2 dashes soy sauce
- Pinch of sea salt
- Pinch of freshly ground black pepper
- Generous squeeze of fresh lime juice
- Pinch of celery seeds

Place all ingredients into a cocktail shaker with ice and shake. Pour into a hurricane-style glass over ice. Garnish with lime wedge and celery. Serves 1.

ALSO RECOMMENDED:
Dubliners. Fifteen easy-to-read tales of human emotion, many only a few pages long, published in 1914 but still relevant today. Insightful and elegantly written; an absolute delight.

JAMAICA KINCAID

The Autobiography of My Mother

Jamaica Kincaid was born Elaine Potter Richardson in 1949 in relative poverty on the island of Antigua in the British West Indies. She was very close to her mother until three younger brothers were born in quick succession and Kincaid began to feel neglected. A permanent rift formed between the author and her mother, who had been her sole caregiver. Of her early life, Kincaid has said that the solitary reading of books, often beneath the front steps of her house, among lizards and bugs, was her sole source of comfort and inspiration.

She received a solid education in Antigua, then still a British colony, but her mother made her leave school at seventeen and sent her to work in Manhattan as an au pair to help support her family. Kincaid, however, refused to send money home or respond to letters from home. She worked at a magazine for teen girls in New York City under the name Jamaica Kincaid and soon became a staff writer at *The New Yorker*, where the editor William Shawn helped nurture her literary gift into full fruition.

In 1979, she married Shawn's son, Allen. They settled in Vermont and had two children. Kincaid converted to Judaism, his faith, although he was not observant. Years after their divorce in 2002, she wrote *See Now Then*, a clear-eyed portrait of a harrowing divorce much like her own. She remains in the house they shared, and still holds to her Judaism.

From *The Autobiography of My Mother*:
"My mother died at the moment I was born, and so for my whole life there was nothing standing between myself and eternity; at my back was always a bleak, black wind."

RUM CHOCOLATE MARTINI

Jamaica Kincaid is an Antiguan American novelist born in St. John's, Antigua. A special Christmastime drink in Antigua is the sweet Ponche Kuba Cream Liqueur.

- 2 oz. Ponche Kuba Cream Liqueur
- 2 oz. chocolate liqueur
- Grated dark chocolate (it's good for you!)
- Ice

Pour liqueurs into a cocktail shaker with ice. Shake and strain into a martini glass. Garnish with grated chocolate. Serves 1.

ALSO RECOMMENDED:
Annie John. A haunting coming-of-age story about an adored only child growing up on the island of Antigua that illustrates Kincaid's exquisite prose.

JHUMPA LAHIRI

The Namesake

Born to Bengali parents in London in 1967, Jhumpa Lahiri grew up in Rhode Island. Her father, a university librarian, and her mother, a schoolteacher, were traditional people; their marriage was arranged, they revered their native land and customs, and never felt at home in America. Jhumpa dressed in jeans and was desperate to assimilate. The family made frequent trips to Calcutta, which reinforced Lahiri's sense that she belonged to neither place.

Lahiri started writing while still in grade school and later worked on the school paper. But even after studying English at Barnard, she felt unworthy to embrace her writing self. Instead, she remained in academia, completing multiple master's degrees and a PhD in Renaissance studies at Boston University.

Her writing career proper began in 1997, when she began a fellowship at the Fine Arts Work Center in Providence. Within two years she secured representation and saw the publication of her short story collection, *Interpreter of Maladies*, for which she was awarded the Pulitzer Prize for fiction, a first for an Indian woman.

The following year she married Alberto Vourvoulias-Bush, a journalist of Guatemalan/Greek American descent, in a traditional Bengali wedding in Calcutta's Singhi Palace. They live in Brooklyn, New York, with their children, Octavio and Noor.

From *The Namesake*:

"On a sticky August evening two weeks before her due date, Ashima Ganguli stands in the kitchen of a Central Square apartment, combining Rice Krispies and Planters peanuts and chopped red onion in a bowl. She adds salt, lemon juice, thin slices of green chili pepper, wishing there were mustard oil to pour into the mix...Even now that there is barely space inside her, it is the one thing she craves."

CLASSIC CHAMPAGNE COCKTAIL

At their wedding, which is not the blissful event most newlyweds typically hope for, the *Namesake* characters Nikhil and Moushumi drink champagne.

1 sugar cube

2–3 dashes Angostura bitters

Champagne

1 oz. brandy

Orange slice for garnish

Maraschino cherry for garnish

Place a sugar cube in the bottom of a Champagne flute. Use the dashes of bitters to saturate the cube. Add the brandy. Fill with Champagne and garnish with a twist of lemon or orange and a cherry. Serves 1.

ALSO RECOMMENDED:
Unaccustomed Earth. A collection of eight transcendent, exquisitely written stories about the secrets of family life.

WALLY LAMB

I Know This Much Is True

Born into a close-knit, working-class Catholic family in Connecticut in 1950, Wally Lamb first developed a love of storytelling from hearing stories at family gatherings. When he was a boy, he wrote and illustrated his own comic books, but the urge to write seriously didn't strike him until he was thirty-two and was inspired by the birth of his son. Realizing the complexity of the task, he applied to a graduate writing program at Vermont College. There he met his mentor, Gladys Swann, whose advice prompted Lamb's deep exploration of Joseph Campbell's writings on mythology. After graduating, Lamb returned to his hometown and taught English at his old high school.

Published in 1992, his first novel, *She's Come Undone*, is set in a fictional Connecticut town and stars an extremely obese but resilient and determined forty-year-old heroine. It became a phenomenon five years later, when selected for Oprah's Book Club (as was his later novel, *I Know This Much Is True*).

In addition to writing his popular and award-winning fiction, Lamb—the father of three boys—teaches at a women's prison.

From *I Know This Much Is True*:
"When you're the sane brother of a schizophrenic identical twin, the tricky thing about saving yourself is the blood it leaves on your hands—the little inconvenience of the look-alike corpse at your feet. And if you're into both survival of the fittest *and* being your brother's keeper—if you've promised your dying mother—then say so long to sleep and hello to the middle of the night."

MANHATTAN

In *I Know This Much Is True*, First Lady Mamie Eisenhower had a photo taken with four-year-old twins Dominick and Thomas and then ordered a Manhattan.

- **3/4 oz. sweet vermouth**
- **2½ oz. bourbon**
- **1 dash Angostura bitters**
- **1 maraschino cherry**
- **1 orange peel**

Rub the cut edge of the orange peel over the glass rim. Combine vermouth, bourbon whiskey, and bitters with ice in a mixing glass. Stir gently, don't bruise the spirits and cloud the drink. Place cherry in a chilled cocktail glass and strain the mixture over it. Serves 1.

ALSO RECOMMENDED:

She's Come Undone. In this novel, Dolores Price is thirteen, wise-mouthed, and wounded. She watches TV, over-eats, and finally enters young womanhood at 257 pounds. Can she get her life back on track?

JOAN STEINAU LESTER

Mama's Child

Joan Steinau Lester grew up working class in New England, yet with her love for smoking French cigarettes, she said she felt at least superficially sophisticated. Despite playing truant in school, she was an excellent student, and skipped a grade to enter college early.

In 1962, at nineteen, she fell in love with an African American scholar and writer. Her family disapproved, so she ran away to New York City and six months later they were married—interracial marriage was illegal in twenty-seven states—and later had two children. Lester cited Doris Lessing's *The Golden Notebook*, published that year, as the book that most influenced her writing. Though she had always considered herself a writer, her only writing while raising kids and editing her husband's work was a journal she kept.

Eventually she divorced her husband and, in 1981, met her longtime partner, Carole Johnson, whom she married in 2008. Lester had begun writing in major news outlets, and a publisher suggested compiling a collection of those pieces, published in 1994 as *The Future of White Men and Other Diversity Dilemmas*.

Her second and third books were also non-fiction (*Taking Charge* and *Fire in My Soul*, the latter a biography of U.S. Rep. Eleanor Holmes Norton). Then her own children's experiences inspired her first novel, *Black, White, Other: In Search of Nina Armstrong*, which was then followed in 2013 by *Mama's Child*.

From *Mama's Child*:
"Her legs had grown so long, so fast—at five-foot-seven she was nearly my height—that every pair of pants she owned were highwater... These days she'd turned mercurial: one moment she was beaming at me, the next I had to grill her to get one scrap of information."

CHIANTI SANGRIA

Lizzie, the mother of Ruby Jordan in *Mama's Child*, is fond of Chianti.

- 3 cups Chianti or other fruity red wine
- 1 cup brandy
- 1/4 cup orange flavored liqueur (recommended: Triple Sec)
- 1 orange, sliced
- 1 lemon, sliced, optional
- 8 fresh strawberries
- Mint
- 2 cups club soda, chilled

In a large pitcher, combine all ingredients except club soda. Cover tightly and refrigerate 3 hours to let flavors meld. Pour ¾ cup sangria mixture into each of eight wine or lowball glasses, dividing fruit equally. Top each glass with ¼ cup club soda. Serve immediately. Serves 8.

ALSO RECOMMENDED:

Black, White, Other: In Search of Nina Armstrong. Nina, a biracial teen whose parents divorce, is stranded in the nowhere land between racial boundaries and the struggle for personal independence.

ALISON LURIE

The Last Resort

Making up stories was the supreme joy of Alison Lurie's young life. Growing up in White Plains, New York, Lurie felt her disadvantages acutely. A birth injury damaged her hearing and left her with facial paralysis, making her mouth turn downward on one side. Neither athletic nor eager to please, she felt convinced she would never be a wife or mother, so she set out to do great literary work. Lurie found inspiration in the iconoclastic heroines of *The Wizard of Oz* and the Nancy Drew series, and has returned to children's literature throughout her career.

After graduating from Radcliffe in 1947, she married Jonathan Peale Bishop, a Harvard grad student. They settled first in Amherst, then near Cornell University in Ithaca, New York, for his teaching assignment. Eventually Lurie joined the Cornell faculty and remained there for over three decades. In 1961, she'd published a few poems and short stories but, feeling exhausted by her literary and parenting efforts, she decided to give up writing. The resulting boredom drove her to write a novel simply for fun. Her third novel, *Love and Friendship*, was published in 1962.

Lurie's most celebrated works, such as *The War Between the Tates*, a comedy of manners depicting a disintegrating marriage during the Vietnam War, take place in the world of academia. Her first marriage ended in 1985. Ten years later she married Edward Hower and now divides her time between Ithaca, New York, London, and Key West, Florida. She has three sons.

From *The Last Resort*:
"...as you grow older and the future shrinks, you have only two choices: you can live in the fading past, or, like children do, in the bright full present."

KEY WEST TEQUILA SUNRISE

The Last Resort is set in Key West, known for its Tequila Sunrises.

> 2 oz. tequila
>
> Orange juice
>
> 2 dashes grenadine syrup
>
> Slice of blood orange
>
> Ice

Pour tequila in a highball glass with ice, and top with orange juice. Stir. Add grenadine by tilting glass and pouring grenadine down the side by flipping the bottle vertically very quickly. The grenadine should go straight to the bottom and then rise up slowly through the drink. Garnish with a slice of blood orange. Serves 1.

ALSO RECOMMENDED:

Foreign Affairs. Virginia Miner, a fifty-something unmarried professor living in London to work on her new book about children's folk rhymes, is drawn into an affair with an Oklahoman tourist. A poignant, witty winner of the Pulitzer Prize for Fiction.

KATHERINE MANSFIELD

The Collected Stories of Katherine Mansfield

A cellist and a gifted singer, Katherine Mansfield, born in 1888, was always writing as well. She found New Zealand, her birthplace, stultifying, so she wrote in her journals of feeling alienated, and of how she had become disillusioned because of the repression of the Maori people. (Maori characters are often portrayed in a sympathetic or positive light in her later stories.) With £100 a year from her father, she was able to escape New Zealand when she was nineteen, never to return—though she kept that world alive in some of her best stories.

Mansfield was a true bohemian. Her lovers included both men and women and, in 1909, pregnant by one man, she married another, left him after a day, miscarried, and began a lesbian relationship with her girlhood friend Ida Baker, who would play an important role throughout Mansfield's life. She called Baker her "wife."

Mansfield finally married the writer/editor John Middleton Murry in 1918; briefly and disastrously, they shared a semi-communal arrangement with D. H. Lawrence and his wife.

In 1923, Mansfield died at thirty-five after a fatal hemorrhage. Murry immediately published her posthumous works, editing her journals, and presenting an idealized version of her as a tragic and beautiful spirit. Virginia Woolf said that Mansfield was the only writer she was jealous of.

From *The Collected Stories of Katherine Mansfield*:
"And after all the weather was ideal. They could not have had a more perfect day for a garden-party if they had ordered it. Windless, warm, the sky without a cloud. Only the blue was veiled with a haze of light gold, as it is sometimes in early summer."

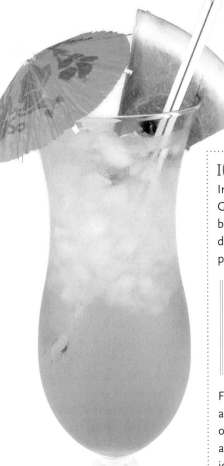

ICED PASSION FRUIT

In one of her short stories, "The Garden Party," Laura, pressured by her family to overcome her distress, offers arriving guests passion-fruit ices.

- **4 oz. mango passion fruit sorbet vodka**
- **1 oz. passion fruit liqueur**
- **Crushed ice**
- **1 slice watermelon**

Fill a shaker with ice cubes. Add all ingredients except watermelon slice. Shake and strain into a tall glass filled with crushed ice. Garnish with watermelon. Serves 1.

ALSO RECOMMENDED:
"Prelude." A key figure in the Modernist movement, Katherine Mansfield perfected the art of the short story. One of her most important works, "Prelude," established her reputation as a master of short fiction.

ALICE MUNRO

Runaway

In her writing, Alice Munro frequently returns to the rough landscape of her childhood in Wingham, Ontario. Of her mother, Munro has said, "My mother...is still a main figure in my life because her life was so sad and unfair and she so brave, but also because she was determined to make me into the Sunday-school-recitation little girl that I was, from the age of seven or so, fighting not to be."

Although she loved getting lost in novels, she was continually frustrated by her inability to complete one of her own. A short story she wrote based on the death of her mother in 1959, when Munro was twenty-eight, was the turning point. After that, she stopped wanting to write novels and embraced the short-story form.

For many years Munro worked in obscurity. When Munro finally published a collection of works, it comprised stories written over fifteen years, while performing household duties and raising three daughters. In 1972, Munro and her husband divorced, which spurred her to attain self-sufficiency through writing.

Munro married Gerald Fremlin in 1976. They lived together until his death in 2013. She has stated emphatically that *Dear Life*, her most recent collection of stories, will be her last. In 2013, Munro won the Nobel Prize in Literature.

From *Runaway*:
"The problem was that she was a girl. If she got married—which might happen, as she was not bad-looking for a scholarship girl, she was not bad-looking at all—she would waste all her hard work and theirs, and if she did not get married she would probably become bleak and isolated, losing out on promotions to men (who needed them more, as they had to support families)."

JULIET'S TIA MARIA

In the short story, "Chance" (from the collection, *Runaway*), Juliet drinks Tia Maria in Eric's bright kitchen, alone, on one of the longest days of the year.

- 1 cup water
- 3/4–1 cup brown sugar
- 4 tsp. powdered coffee
- 1 cup rum
- 4 tsp. vanilla extract
- Caramel sauce
- Whipped cream

Boil water, sugar, and coffee for ten minutes. Let cool. Add rum and vanilla. Pour into a bottle and refrigerate for one week before serving. To serve, pour into a martini glass and top with whipped cream and a drizzle of caramel sauce. Serves 2–3.

ALSO RECOMMENDED:
Dear Life. Through flawed and fully human characters, Alice Munro pinpoints the moment a person is forever altered by a chance encounter, an action not taken, or a simple twist of fate.

FLANNERY O'CONNOR

A Good Man is Hard to Find and Other Stories

O'Connor was born in Savannah in 1925 and raised a Catholic. Her father died of lupus; her mother ran a dairy farm in Milledgeville, Georgia. Flannery was a wild, brilliant only child. When she was five, she taught a pet chicken to walk backward.

After college, she enrolled in the then-new Iowa Writers' Workshop, and in 1950 she became ill with lupus and moved back to her mother's farm. Many of her stories, in particular, are considered powerful tragicomic masterpieces of the Southern Gothic tradition. O'Connor was eccentric herself; she put Coca-Cola in her coffee and once gave her mother a mule for Mother's Day.

She had many friends, but her only romance was a brief liaison (exactly one kiss) with a textbook salesman; she also had a long-distance friendship with a fan, a lonely lesbian woman with whom she exchanged more than 300 letters.

Later in life, her mother took her to Lourdes, hoping Flannery's lupus would be cured. It was not. Close to death at age thirty-nine, when asked if she heard the celestial choir, she said yes, but it was singing "Clementine."

O'Connor wrote little, but her life was so short and her health so broken that her output is actually amazing: thirty-one stories, two novels, and hundreds of entertaining letters.

From "A Good Man is Hard to Find," in *Flannery O'Connor: Collected Works*:
"The boy's look was irritated but dogged. 'I don't care,' he said. "I don't care a thing about what all you done. I just want to know if you love me or don'tcher?' and he caught her to him and wildly planted her face with kisses until she said, 'Yes, yes.'"

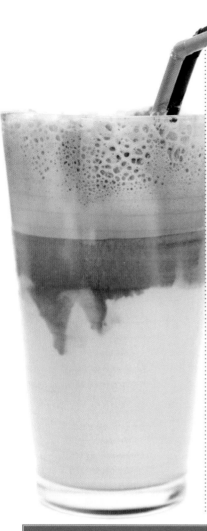

SALTED CARAMEL & BOURBON MILK SHAKE

In the short story, "Wise Blood," Enoch drinks a chocolate malted milk shake whilst making suggestive remarks to the waitress whom he believes to be in love with him.

- 3 big scoops vanilla ice cream
- 2 oz. bourbon
- 1/3 cup caramel sauce, plus 2 tbsp. for garnish
- 1 cup milk
- ½ tsp. salt
- Ice cubes

Place milk, salt, caramel sauce, and ice in a blender and pulse to combine, until frothy. Add ice cream and bourbon and pulse until incorporated. Pour into a serving glass and top with remaining caramel sauce. Serves 1.

ALSO RECOMMENDED:
Everything That Rises Must Converge. A collection of short stories published posthumously in 1965. The title story was awarded the O. Henry Prize in short fiction in 1963, the second of three O. Henry Prizes received by O'Connor.

JOYCE CAROL OATES

After the Wreck, I Picked Myself Up,
Spread My Wings, and Flew Away

Joyce Carol Oates (pseudonyms Rosamond Smith and Lauren Kelly) was born on a farm in Lockport, New York, in 1938, the oldest of three children. Her parents had both grown up impoverished, but her own childhood was, she stresses, unremarkable. As a teenager, she was given a typewriter and a copy of *Alice's Adventures in Wonderland*. She wrote her first novel a year later. After winning a scholarship to Syracuse University and then a major fiction contest, Oates married a fellow grad student, Raymond Smith, and they settled in Detroit, where they worked as teachers.

Oates's own life was marked by the violence that has become a characteristic of her fiction. She was especially shattered to learn that the father of her paternal grandmother, a gravedigger, had committed suicide with a shotgun, an event that inspired her novel *The Gravedigger's Daughter*.

Oates's many published works range from historical novels to poetry to a lengthy study of boxing. She's says there's no mystery to her productivity. An early riser, she often finishes a novel, then starts a new project while revising the old one.

Oates teaches at Princeton and lives nearby in a house she shared with Smith until he died, unexpectedly, in 2008. Her 2001 memoir, *A Widow's Story*, describes her intense grieving. However, she was remarried in 2009, to Charles Gross, a fellow professor.

From *After the Wreck, I Picked Myself Up, Spread My Wings, and Flew Away*:
"'Jenna, hey. You are one hell of a girl.' I guess. I wanted to think so. Dragging my feet, which felt like lead. But I was on my feet, the nurses were amazed."

ZOMBIE COLA

In *After the Wreck*, Jenna and her friend Trina drink Zombie Colas, diet cola with vodka.

> **2 oz. vodka**
>
> **Diet cola**
>
> **1 lemon wheel**

Pour vodka into a tall glass with ice. Top with diet cola. Garnish with a lemon wheel. Serves 1.

ALSO RECOMMENDED:
Small Avalanches and Other Stories. Twelve intense stories that explore the dark, enigmatic psyche of the teenage years in this sometimes unnerving, sometimes uplifting collection.

DOROTHY PARKER

The Poetry & Short Stories of Dorothy Parker

Dorothy Parker was born in 1893. Before she reached the age of fourteen, her mother, stepmother, and father were dead, and her uncle had gone down on the *Titanic*. She was impoverished and forced to earn her living.

One of her major achievements, in her twenties, was to help found the Round Table, a group of writers famous for their wit, irreverence, and intellectual brilliance, at New York City's Algonquin Hotel. Many of Parker's witticisms have become famous, including (regarding a well-known actress): "She ran the whole gamut of emotions from A to B."

By the time *The New Yorker* was launched (1925), Parker had a formidable reputation and the magazine was quick to publish her. Her award-winning stories were unlike her light-hearted poetry: dark, angry, and intolerant of pretension.

After many affairs, she finally divorced her stockbroker husband, married another writer, and moved to Hollywood, where they collaborated on numerous screenplays, including *A Star Is Born*. When investigated by the House Un-American Activities Committee in the fifties and called upon to testify, Parker took the Fifth and was promptly blacklisted.

Later, Parker, a heavy drinker, was depressed and in poor health; she lasted until the age of seventy-three, when she died of a heart attack. She bequeathed her estate to the Dr. Martin Luther King Jr. Foundation.

From *The Poetry & Short Stories of Dorothy Parker:*
"She had gowns of velvet like poured country cream and satin with the lacquer of buttercups and chiffon that spiraled about her like golden smoke. She wore them, and listened in shy surprise to the resulting comparisons to daffodils, and butterflies in the sunshine, and such; but she knew."

CHAMPAGNE BELLINI

The only female founding member of the Algonquin Round Table was known for her love of champagne and famously said "Three be the things I shall never attain: Envy, content, and sufficient champagne."

> **2 oz. peach puree (or peach juice)**
>
> **Champagne**

Pour the peach juice or peach puree into a Champagne flute. Slowly add the Champagne. Serves 1.

ALSO RECOMMENDED:
Dorothy Parker—Complete Stories. Dorothy Parker's talents extended far beyond brash one-liners and clever rhymes. Her stories laid bare the uncertainties and disappointments of ordinary people living ordinary lives.

KATHERINE ANNE PORTER

The Collected Stories of Katherine Anne Porter

Katherine Porter was born in the tiny town of India Creek, Texas, in 1890. Her mother died when Porter was two and her childhood was difficult, though she did grow up with books and culture. She escaped into marriage at age sixteen to a railway porter who beat her; they divorced after ten years, and she worked as an actress, singer, drama critic, and gossip columnist. She nearly died during the 1918 influenza epidemic, a brush with death that turned her hair white. Her powerful novella *Pale Horse, Pale Rider* (1940) drew on this harrowing experience.

In her twenties, she settled in Greenwich Village and began to publish stories. She continued to succumb to bad marriages, one to a deadly dull man from Connecticut (after a miserable year, she sneaked out early one morning to catch a train back to New York), and her last to a graduate student who discovered during the wedding that she was twenty years his senior. They were often taken for mother and son, the marriage was a complete disaster, and they were quickly divorced.

Unable to bear children after a hysterectomy, Porter directed her energies toward her dark, meticulously crafted, and increasingly acclaimed stories. She eventually won both a Pulitzer and a National Book Award. Her enormously successful only novel, *Ship of Fools* (1962), with its half-million-dollar movie sale, brought her the first financial stability of her life.

From *Pale Horse, Pale Rider*, in *The Collected Stories of Katherine Anne Porter*:
"I don't want to love," she would think in spite of herself, "not Adam, there is no time and we are not ready for it and yet this is all we have..."

ORANGE CHAMPAGNE PUNCH

In *Pale Horse, Pale Rider*, when Miranda is ill, Adam brings her orange juice and takes care of her.

- **1 cup fresh orange juice**
- **1 cup maraschino cherry juice**
- **1/2 cup dark rum**
- **1/2 cup brandy**
- **1 bottle chilled Champagne**
- **Lime peel for garnish**
- **Maraschino cherry for garnish**

In a large punch bowl or pitcher stir orange juice, cherry juice, rum, and brandy to blend. Refrigerate thirty minutes. Add Champagne just before serving. Garnish with lime peel and cherry. Serves 6.

ALSO RECOMMENDED:
Ship of Fools. Porter's only novel, published when she was seventy-two, follows a group of cruise ship passengers bound for Germany in 1931, and represents society at large in that era.

MATTHEW QUICK

The Silver Linings Playbook

Matthew Quick always wanted to be an author, but in his family in Oaklyn, New Jersey, reading was not encouraged and a literary career deemed unmanly. An isolated teenager and fan of the bands the Smiths and the Cure, Quick concealed his inner turmoil. He adored reading—Kurt Vonnegut's *Slaughterhouse-Five* was an early favorite—and eventually he received some crucial encouragement from high school teachers. He was all-too-happy to escape the confines of his hometown when he entered La Salle University, Philadelphia, Pennsylvania, in 1992.

After graduation, he became a tenured, well-loved English teacher, sports coach, and youth counselor at an upscale South Jersey high school, while his wife, a fellow fiction writer, taught at Bryn Mawr College. Because teaching was time-consuming, they both put aside their careers in 2004 to pursue writing—a difficult decision that Quick credits with sustaining both his marriage and his livelihood. He pursued an MFA in creative writing at Goddard College.

After Quick had written two novels and a creative thesis, his mentor remarked that his work lacked humor, so he decided to write something unashamedly entertaining. It became *Silver Linings Playbook,* which, after being discovered among unsolicited manuscript submissions at a high-end literary agency, became a bestseller and the basis for an Oscar-winning film.

Quick and his wife, Alicia Bessette, live in Massachusetts.

From *The Silver Linings Playbook*:
"I don't have to look up to know Mom is making another surprise visit. Her toenails are always pink during the summer months, and I recognize the flower design imprinted on her leather sandals; it's what Mom purchased the last time she signed me out of the bad place and took me to the mall."

BEER MARGARITA

In the *Silver Linings Playbook*, Pat, the protagonist, after performing a choreographed dance with Tiffany, goes to an epic tailgating party and drinks beer.

> 2–12 oz. bottles of your favorite beer, chilled
>
> 1/2 cup limeade (frozen concentrate, thawed)
>
> 1/2 cup tequila (chilled)
>
> Crushed ice
>
> Fig wedges

In a pitcher, combine beer, limeade, and tequila. Fill glasses with crushed ice, then with margarita mixture. Optional: Garnish with fig wedges and serve. Serves 4.

ALSO RECOMMENDED:
Forgive Me, Leonard Peacock. An unflinching, moving examination of impossible choices facing an eighteen-year-old boy who hides a gun in his backpack.

NINA SANKOVITCH

Tolstoy and the Purple Chair

Nina Sankovitch was born in Evanston, Illinois, the third daughter of immigrant parents. Her father escaped the fate of his three siblings, who were murdered in Belarus during World War II.

Nina's family adored books. Her mother, a Belgian, taught French literature; her middle sister, Natasha, is a professor of comparative literature. Her father eased his slow recuperation from tuberculosis by reading novels out loud. From an early age, Nina turned to books for solace and guidance.

After graduating from Tufts University, Sankovitch earned a law degree from Harvard in 1987 and worked in corporate law. Even as a lawyer, she would often close her office door to read books.

In 2005 her older sister, Anne-Marie, died of bile duct cancer, and Sankovitch was devastated. After three years, still grief-stricken, she decided to work through her grief by reading a book a day in an effort to learn how people in books dealt with bereavement, and chronicled her progress on her website, readallday.org. Along with novels and mysteries, she covered a breadth of styles, including humor, musical oral history, and books on grief. The project earned positive press and a book deal. *Tolstoy and the Purple Chair* established her literary reputation and allayed some of her despair.

Sankovitch lives in Westport, Connecticut, with her husband and four sons— ages eight through sixteen— all voracious readers.

From *Tolstoy and the Purple Chair*:
"My year of reading was my own hiatus, my own suspension in time between the overwhelming sorrow of my sister's death and the future that now waits before me. During my yearlong respite filled with books, I recuperated. Even more, I learned how to move beyond recuperation to living."

TOLSTOY AND THE PURPLE CHAIR*

Nina created this recipe in honor of Tolstoy and all the books she read in her purple chair.

| **6 oz. Prosecco Rosato (sparkling rose wine)**
| **2 oz. Hpnotiq**
| **2 oz. cranberry juice**
| **Lemon peels**

Pour chilled Prosecco and Hpnotiq into a daiquiri glass and top up with chilled cranberry juice. Garnish with strips of lemon peel. Serves 2.

*As made on BookGirlTV interview with Nina Sankovitch.

ALSO RECOMMENDED:
Signed, Sealed, Delivered: Celebrating the Joys of Letter Writing. After finding a trove of old letters in her apartment, Nina explores what's special about the handwritten letter.

DANI SHAPIRO

Devotion

Daneile Joyce Shapiro was born in New York City in 1962 to Jewish parents who converted to orthodoxy. Her father was a financier, her mother a psychotherapist. As a child she studied at a yeshiva and was fluent in Hebrew. In her teens she attended Pingry, a New Jersey prep school. A capable, confident student, she also acted in TV commercials from childhood through her teens.

As an undergraduate at Sarah Lawrence College, Shapiro studied with Grace Paley, an experience that influenced her writing greatly, as did her graduate work there. During this time she secured representation for her first novel, *Playing With Fire*. With its elements of wealth and traditional Judaism, it drew upon Shapiro's traditional upbringing and subsequent rebellion.

Around this time she began teaching creative writing, at an offshoot of Yeshiva University, where her first students were orthodox Jewish girls who were having doubts about the future.

She published two more novels, but it was the memoir *Slow Motion*—an unflinching account of her years as the kept woman of a friend's rich father—that garnered wide acclaim.

In 1997 she married Michael Maren, a journalist and screenwriter. (Her previous marriage ended in divorce.) Shortly after their son was born, they moved to Connecticut, where they still live.

From *Devotion*:
"It was the first day of Rosh Hashanah, and many years had passed since I had last set foot in a synagogue, much less participated in this ritual called *tashlich*, which follows the long Rosh Hashanah service. I dragged myself to the Shepaug River, fighting my own resistance every step of the way. I had better things to do."

CARAMEL APPLE MARTINI*

During Rosh Hashanah, apples are dipped in honey because they symbolize Gan Eden (the Garden of Eden) and they're sweet, symbolic of the sweet year that is hopefully ahead.

- **2 oz. butterscotch schnapps**
- **2 oz. Sour Apple Pucker**
- **1 oz. vodka**
- **3 slices green apple**

Shake ingredients, except apple slices, in a cocktail shaker with ice. Strain into a chilled martini glass. Garnish with sliced apples. Serves 1.

*As made on BookGirlTV interview with Dani Shapiro.

ALSO RECOMMENDED:

Still Writing: The Pleasures and Perils of a Writing Life. Lessons learned from the writing life; an intimate and eloquent guide to living a creative life.

MARY SHELLEY

Frankenstein

Mary Shelley's parents were the radical political philosopher William Godwin and the feminist writer Mary Wollstonecraft (who died within days of her daughter's birth). Precocious in every way, Mary met Percy Bysshe Shelley, the Romantic poet, philosopher and passionate atheist (who was already married) in 1812, when she was fifteen and he twenty. To the dismay of their families and friends, they eloped, risking ostracism from society. (They kept a joint journal of their travels, published on their return a few years later.) Their first child (of a total of four) died after twelve days. Shelley was the heir to a baronetcy in Sussex, and in 1815 his grandfather died and left him enough to live on.

During a rainy visit to their friend the poet Byron at Lake Geneva, Byron challenged his guests to a contest: who could write the best tale of the supernatural? Mary's contribution, *Frankenstein*, grew out of a vision of "the hideous phantasm of a man stretched out, and then, on the working of some powerful engine, showed signs of life, and stirred..."

In 1816, after Shelley's estranged wife drowned herself, he and Mary were finally married. They lived in Italy until Shelley died in 1822. Mary returned to London with her son, their only child to live past the age of three. She was a writer all her life, but *Frankenstein*, published when she was twenty-one, is by far her best-known work.

From *Frankenstein*:

"The old man, whom I soon perceived to be blind, employed his leisure hours on his instrument or in contemplation. Nothing could exceed the love and respect which the younger cottagers exhibited towards their venerable companion."

FRANKENSTEIN'S BERRY PUNCH

When Frankenstein's monster was roaming the woods, he lived on acorns and berries.

- 2 cups pomegranate juice (chilled)
- 1 cup cranberry juice (chilled)
- 1 cup vodka
- 1 cup Cointreau liqueur
- 1 cup club soda (chilled)
- 1/2 cup fresh lemon juice (from 6 lemons)
- 1/2 cup simple syrup
- 1/2 pint raspberries and blackberries
- Ice cubes

Combine pomegranate juice, cranberry juice, vodka, Cointreau, club soda, lemon juice, and simple syrup in a punch bowl with ice. Fill glasses with blackberries and raspberries. Serves 4–6.

ALSO RECOMMENDED:
The Last Man. This 1826 novel reflects Shelley's fears about civilization and the shortcomings of human behavior as she scrutinizes politics and philosophy and reflects upon pitfalls of human behavior.

SANDI KAHN SHELTON

Kissing Games of the World

Sandi Kahn Shelton's family life was steeped in the Southern storytelling tradition. Growing up in Jacksonville, Florida, she learned quickly that the best way to command her family's attention was by spinning a good yarn. When she wrote a story and sold it to some neighbors in exchange for ice cream money, it put her on a path toward a writing life, although not a straight one.

After her first marriage ended, she took a job as a writer at the *New Haven Register*. When she found that most of her colleagues had no inkling of what life as a single parent was like, she began writing a column and started a novel too, but her journalism and parenting obligations meant that she could only work on the latter sporadically. Seventeen years passed before the book was published. The deadpan wit of *What Comes After Crazy* earned the author comparisons to Erma Bombeck, the ultimate American voice of harried housewifery.

After two more novels with thirty-something protagonists, Kahn Shelton wanted to write about women at a later stage of life, with other concerns beyond falling madly in love. She wrote these books under the pseudonym Maddie Dawson.

A longtime Connecticut resident, she lives with her husband, Jim Shelton, and their three children. She teaches creative writing and is working on her next novel.

From *Kissing Games of the World:*
"He'd tell anyone: if you want to stay young, keep up with a toddler when you're in your sixties. That'll either kill you or keep you going. For him, it had been the tonic he needed, saved him from all the guilt that gnawed away at his insides."

BETWEEN THE SHEETS*
Chosen in honor of Jamie, whose bed is where the grandfather in this fun novel meets an untimely end.

> 3/4 oz. brandy
> 3/4 oz. rum
> 1 oz. Cointreau
> 1/2 oz. lemon juice
> Olive

Pour all ingredients except olive into a cocktail shaker filled with ice. Shake well. Strain into a chilled cocktail glass and garnish with olive. Serves 1.

*As made on BookGirlTV video interview with Sandi Kahn Shelton.

ALSO RECOMMENDED:
The Stuff That Never Happened (written as Maddie Dawson). Offered a second chance at an unforgettable love, Annabelle McKay must decide between a man she loves and the husband who has stood squarely by her side.

ELIZABETH TAYLOR

Complete Short Stories of Elizabeth Taylor

Often called "the other Elizabeth Taylor," the non-actress Taylor was underrated during her lifetime, though after her death, Kingsley Amis called her "one of the best English novelists born in this century," and her short stories today are considered classics.

Pathologically shy, Taylor, born in 1912, became a governess and a librarian before she married and lived an upper-middle-class existence in a small Buckinghamshire town. Of her life, she once said, "Nothing sensational, thank heavens, has ever happened." But a few surprises turned up: her liberal politics (including an early flirtation with communism), an occasional bet on the ponies, and a twelve-year affair with a painter named Ray Russell.

She met Russell soon after she was married, and wrote him dozens of letters during their romance, many of which (at her request) he burned. But her secret life was eventually discovered and her husband insisted she end the affair. She did.

Taylor wrote twelve novels, four short-story collections, and one children's book. Her fiction focuses on the daily lives of characters who could have come from her own genteel social milieu. But she was unsentimental and bitingly witty, with a keen eye for human foibles and a wonderful ear for dialogue. Her humor is sly, and her acerbic social comedies hint at rage and violence seething just below the surface.

From "A Sad Garden," in *Complete Short Stories*:
"The garden was filled with the smell of rotting fruit. Pears lay about on the paths and wasps tunneled into their ripeness. Audrey stepped timidly over them. She was all white and clean-face, serge coat and socks. Her mother held the William pear in her gloved hand. 'You shall have it when we get home,' she promised."

PEAR SMASH

As noted in the excerpt from the exquisite short story, "A Sad Garden," pears lie where they've fallen on the path, rotting as wasps tunnel into their ripeness. This recipe puts such ripe pears to good use—before the wasps can get them!

> 1½ oz. pear flavored vodka
>
> 1½ oz. pear nectar
>
> 1/4 oz. fresh lemon juice
>
> Splash of soda
>
> Pear chunk, cut one inch thick

Put vodka, pear nectar, and lemon juice into a cocktail shaker with ice cubes and shake well. Pour into a glass and top off with soda. Garnish with pear chunk. Serves 1.

ALSO RECOMMENDED:
Mrs. Palfrey at the Claremont. When the widowed Mrs. Palfrey arrives at the Claremont Hotel, where she will spend her remaining days, she meets eccentric characters and strikes up an unexpected friendship with a handsome young writer.

CHRISTINA THOMPSON

*Come on Shore and We Will Kill and Eat
You All: A New Zealand Story*

The daughter of a professor, Christina Thompson read widely and deeply from an early age, making her way from C. S. Lewis through Tolstoy and Flaubert and ultimately finding her greatest influence, Joseph Conrad, "a Pole who thought in French and wrote in English."

After college, prompted by the alluring Outback vistas being served up by the Australian film industry of the early 1980s, she applied for a fellowship at the University of Melbourne.

Thompson began writing, mostly book reviews and academic papers. She yearned to write more creatively, but had no interest in short stories or novels. During her graduate work, which looked at indigenous Pacific peoples and their first contact with Europeans, she made a stopover in New Zealand. There she observed an interracial pub fight and talked with a native Maori man named Seven, whom she would later marry.

The resulting convergence of her own culture with that of her husband found expression in *Come On Shore and We Will Kill and Eat You All*, a hybrid travel book/personal history/anthro-love-story that forced the author to uncover the dark legacy of her own maternal ancestors.

Thompson is also editor of *Harvard Review* and teaches in the Harvard University Extension School. She and her husband and three sons live outside of Boston, where she continues to write.

From *Come on Shore and We Will Kill and Eat You All: A New Zealand Story*:

"'Contact' is what we call it when two previously unacquainted groups meet for the very first time...It describes a moment of sudden wonder, a tectonic shift, that undermines old certainties and opens up whole new views."

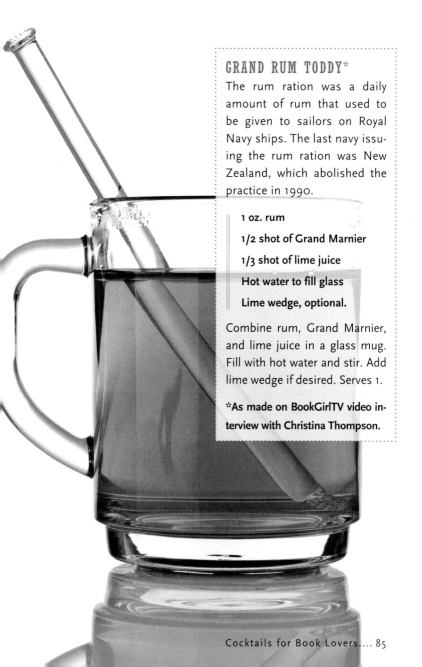

GRAND RUM TODDY*

The rum ration was a daily amount of rum that used to be given to sailors on Royal Navy ships. The last navy issuing the rum ration was New Zealand, which abolished the practice in 1990.

1 oz. rum

1/2 shot of Grand Marnier

1/3 shot of lime juice

Hot water to fill glass

Lime wedge, optional.

Combine rum, Grand Marnier, and lime juice in a glass mug. Fill with hot water and stir. Add lime wedge if desired. Serves 1.

***As made on BookGirlTV video interview with Christina Thompson.**

WILLIAM TREVOR

My House in Umbria

Born William Trevor Cox in County Cork, Ireland, in 1928, Trevor grew up with two siblings in a tense, silent household with parents who couldn't stand each other. Though Trevor settled in England after college for economic reasons, he proudly embraces his Irish literary heritage and cites the outsider-ness conferred on him by his early Protestantism in Catholic Ireland as a creative gift.

A devourer of mysteries and thrillers by age ten, he moved on to Maugham and Dickens and Irish authors in his teens. As a student, he only distinguished himself in writing, yet his youthful ambition was to follow his father into banking.

In 1952, while at Trinity College, Dublin, Trevor met Jane Ryan, his future wife. Upon graduation, he embarked on a career as a sculptor, then as a schoolteacher. For years he did no writing at all. In 1958 he had a novel published. It failed, forcing him to support himself as an ad-agency copywriter, a job he loathed. It was there that he began writing *Old Boys* (1964), his first proper novel and the one that established the name of William Trevor. The famous English writer Graham Greene declared Trevor's collection *Angels at the Ritz* to be perhaps "the best since James Joyce's *Dubliners.*"

Trevor emphatically insists he is not interested in himself. "Other people interest me far more," he said. "Other people fascinate me." He has won many awards, including the Booker Prize and the Whitbread Award.

The Trevors live in a Victorian farmhouse in the countryside of Devon.

From *My House in Umbria*:
"It is not easy to introduce myself. Gloria Grey, Janine Ann Johns, Cora Lamore: there is a choice, and there have been other names as well. Names hardly matter, I think; it is perhaps enough to say I like Emily Delahunty best."

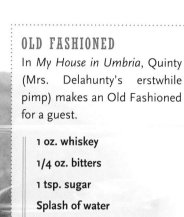

OLD FASHIONED

In *My House in Umbria*, Quinty (Mrs. Delahunty's erstwhile pimp) makes an Old Fashioned for a guest.

- 1 oz. whiskey
- 1/4 oz. bitters
- 1 tsp. sugar
- Splash of water
- 1 orange wheel
- Maraschino cherry

In an old-fashioned glass, muddle sugar, bitters, and water. Add ice cubes. Add whiskey. Garnish with orange wheel and maraschino cherry. Serves 1.

ALSO RECOMMENDED:
Cheating at Canasta. Subtle yet powerful, these exquisitely nuanced tales of regret, deception, adultery, aging, and forgiveness are a rare pleasure, and confirm Trevor's reputation as a master of the short story form.

JOANNA TROLLOPE

Other People's Children

The eldest of three children born to a rector and his wife, Joanna Trollope grew up in the picturesque Cotswolds in the south of England. Driven more by a need to communicate and a love of story than by a sense of literary destiny (she is distantly related to the famous Victorian novelist Anthony Trollope), Joanna started writing as a young girl, producing her first novel in 1957 at the age of fourteen. (She kept it locked away.)

Joanna entered Oxford University on a modest scholarship and there met David Potter, her future husband. They had two daughters, but split acrimoniously after eighteen years together.

One year later, in 1967, Trollope left her job in England's Foreign Office and became a teacher. After the children had gone to bed, she took up writing again, and in 1980 devoted herself to it full-time. Her first published books were historical novels under the name Caroline Harvey.

Trollope married TV screenwriter Ian Curteis in 1985. The following year she wrote her final pseudonymous historical novel, *The Choir*. The first book released under her given name appeared in 1988, followed by a streak of bestselling novels.

Now divorced a second time, Joanna Trollope lives in London, near her family and friends. She still writes in longhand and says writing her books generally takes as long as a pregnancy. In 1996, she was awarded the Officer of the British Empire (OBE) for services to literature.

From *Other People's Children*:
"She glanced toward her daughter. Josie looked so happy, so pretty, in a cream silk suit with her red hair done up somehow behind her head, that it seemed downright unkind to have misgivings."

APRICOT BRANDY COBBLER

In *Other People's Children*, Elizabeth goes to Harrods to buy a pheasant, Stilton cheese, and candied apricots to take down to her father in Bath.

- 1 tsp. superfine sugar
- 3 oz. club soda
- 2 oz. apricot brandy
- 1 maraschino cherry
- 1 orange slice

In an old-fashioned glass, dissolve the sugar in the club soda. Add crushed ice until the glass is almost full. Add the brandy. Stir well. Garnish with the cherry and orange slice. Serves 1.

ALSO RECOMMENDED:
The Soldier's Wife. Dan Riley, a British army major, comes home from Afghanistan to the wife, daughters, and extended family he adores. He's up for promotion. Will his family support his passion for his career?

GAIL TSUKIYAMA

Women of the Silk

Gail Tsukiyama's father was Japanese; born and raised in Oahu, he witnessed the bombing of Pearl Harbor as a child, perched in a tree. Her mother was from Hong Kong. While Gail and her mother took frequent trips to China to see her grandmother, Gail identified as an American while growing up in San Francisco. Her quest to understand her complicated heritage has animated her writing life.

She was a teenage poet, and won awards for her poetry in college, but only began to consider a literary career during graduate work in creative writing.

At first she concentrated on short stories and poetry, but eventually she wanted to try writing a novel with a beginning, a middle, and an end. Because she chose to start with a multigenerational tale set within the Chinese silk trade, and because she got deeply into writing it before starting again from scratch, it took her five years to write. When she finally received the advance hardcover copy of *Women of the Silk*, it was a key moment of personal satisfaction. Published in 1991, this unexpected hit launched her writing career.

Tsukiyama credits good timing for her initial success, coming as it did right after Amy Tan's *Joy Luck Club*. Book publishers were more interested in the work of Asian American women authors than ever before.

Tsukiyama lives in California, in El Cerrito and the Napa Valley. When not writing, she enjoys good red wine, good and bad TV, and shoe shopping.

From *Women of the Silk*:
"Over the years, she had grown as silent as her husband. She had learned to keep all her thoughts to herself. Yu-sung had let go of the spontaneity of her girlhood."

SWEET MULBERRYTINI

In *Women of the Silk*, Pei's family made a living by farming fish and picking mulberry leaves.

> 1 scoop vanilla ice cream
>
> 3 tbsp. vodka
>
> 1 tbsp. dried white mulberries

Put ice cream, vodka, and mulberries in a blender and pulse until smooth. Pour into a martini glass. Serves 1.

ALSO RECOMMENDED:
The Language of Threads. Pei, brought to work in the silk house as a girl, has grown into a determined young woman who, in the 1930s, leaves the silk house for Hong Kong.

ANNE TYLER

Saint Maybe

Anne Tyler was raised in a Quaker community in Raleigh, North Carolina, and once lived on a commune, which instilled in her a sense of distance from the world. At three, she began inventing elaborate stories and reading voraciously. She especially loved Eudora Welty's writing and its depiction of the ordinary. Writing and illustrating a succession of her own books, Tyler imagined she would be an artist.

Entering Duke University at sixteen, in 1957, Tyler took a writing class with the writer Reynolds Price, who helped get her stories published. Notably publicity-shy, she rarely grants interviews and is almost never photographed. Despite her early literary success, once she graduated, Tyler chose not to pursue writing, but Russian studies at Columbia.

In 1963, Tyler married Taghi Modarressi, a child psychiatrist and fiction writer, and they settled in Montreal. Tyler worked as an assistant librarian at McGill University Law School and wrote her two novels, *If Morning Ever Comes* (1964) and *The Tin Can Tree* (1965).

In 1967 she moved to Baltimore and in 1977, told a reporter she never planned to leave the house in Baltimore she shared with her husband and two daughters. Modarressi died of cancer in 1997, but Tyler still lives there. She is now at work on what she says is her final book, a generational family saga told in reverse chronology. The working title is "A Spool of Blue Thread." Anne Tyler's most recent novel is *The Beginner's Goodbye*.

From *Saint Maybe*:
"'They are not the burden I meant. The burden is forgiveness.' 'Okay,' Ian said. 'Fine. How much longer till I'm forgiven?' 'No, no.' [Reverend Emmett replied.] 'The burden is that *you* must forgive.'"

IAN'S CHERRY COLA

In *Saint Maybe*, Ian passes the little snack shop where he and Cicely used to sit all afternoon over a couple of cherry cokes.

| 1 oz. whiskey
| 1 oz. cherry juice
| 1/2 oz. amaretto
| 1/2 oz. ginger brandy
| 2 oz. cherry cola
| 1 maraschino cherry

In a cocktail shaker add whiskey, cherry juice, amaretto, and brandy and shake for fifteen seconds. Pour over ice, then top off with cherry cola and stir. Serve with additional cherries, if desired. Serves 1.

ALSO RECOMMENDED:
Breathing Lessons. Maggie and Ira Moran have been married for twenty-eight years and it shows. Will Maggie and Ira be able to rediscover the magic? (A Pulitzer Prize winner.)

THRITY UMRIGAR

First Darling of the Morning

Thrity Umrigar was born into a middle-class Parsi family in cosmopolitan Bombay (now Mumbai) and brought up in the Zoroastrian (an ancient religious philosophy) faith. As a child, she was deeply affected by the plight of beggars in her city, but was told the condition was inevitable; by her teenage years she realized she could be an agent of change.

Umrigar attended a Catholic school in a mostly Hindu city, where the atmosphere was one of inclusivity. She wrote incessantly as a means of expressing her complicated feelings: Thrity's father was gentle but absent. Her cruel, mocking mother beat her with switches. Her earliest poems took the form of anonymous notes to her parents. By her teens she was committed to writing.

Reading *Midnight's Children*—Salman Rushdie's remembrance of Bombay on the cusp of Indian independence—was both revelation and inspiration for Umrigar. She was also deeply struck by *Lust For Life*, Irving Howe's biography of Vincent Van Gogh, which inspired her to reject her parents' bourgeois existence.

At twenty-one, she left India to study at Ohio State University, and was an established journalist when she met her agent-to-be, serendipitously, at a college lecture; they clicked, and Umrigar began writing chapters that eventually became *Bombay Time*, her acclaimed debut novel of 2001. Having since written four novels and a memoir, she works as a journalist in Cleveland, her longtime home.

From *First Darling of the Morning: Selected Memories of an Indian Childhood*:
"I am of that generation of middle-class, westernized, citified Indian kids who know the words to Do-Re-Me better than the national anthem. *The Sound of Music* is our call to arms and Julie Andrews our Pied Piper."

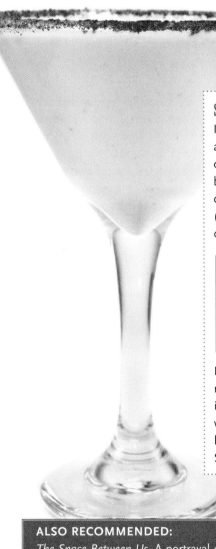

SHERRY ALEXANDER

In *The Space Between Us*, after a warm but misguided moment of love expressed, Sera's husband Feroz takes her out for a drink and she has a Kingfisher (Indian beer) and he has a glass of sherry.

- 1 oz. brandy
- 1 oz. medium dry sherry
- 1 oz. brandy cream
- Splash of heavy cream
- Freshly grated nutmeg

Rim a martini glass with grated nutmeg. Combine all remaining ingredients in a cocktail shaker with ice and shake vigorously. Strain into a martini glass. Serves 1.

ALSO RECOMMENDED:
The Space Between Us. A portrayal of two women who discover an emotional rapport as they struggle against the confines of a rigid caste system in modern India.

HELEN WAN

The Partner Track

Helen Wan is a California-born Chinese American who grew up in Virginia, a capable and eager student whose fifth-grade teacher instilled in her a love of words. After graduating from Amherst College, she earned a law degree and practiced corporate law in New York before finding her way to an entertainment firm. This led her to become in-house counsel at Time, Inc., a position she still holds.

She'd always wanted to write a novel, and had published some essays and reviews of fiction while in law school, but was limited by her lawyerly responsibilities. Finally, when her husband learned he was being transferred to Texas, Wan took a leave of absence and started writing. In the end, they didn't have to relocate, but she was already off and running. That project became *The Partner Track*, published in 2013, the story of a Chinese American corporate lawyer who meets the glass ceiling head-on.

In the end, it took her twelve years to complete, and the road to securing representation led to many sleepless nights. (One agent suggested she rewrite the book but eliminate the protagonist's ethnicity.) Wan finally availed herself of a modern alternative called Query Roulette, a hands-on forum where authors can meet agents and discuss their books face-to-face. From one such event, Wan landed both an agent and a book deal.

She lives with her husband and son in Brooklyn, and is a huge Harry Potter fan.

From *The Partner Track*:
"I could not stop looking and looking out that window, at the deep violet hue spreading across the sky. It felt as if the day's humiliations were draining from my body, and I was waking up fresh."

SLUGGER'S BIG APPLE SANGRIA*

Ingrid (aka "Slugger") relaxed with a glass of Pinot Grigio after a hard day at the office.

- 1 bottle white wine
- 1 Red Delicious apple, sliced thin
- 1/2 bottle of champagne or sparkling wine, chilled

Pour wine into a pitcher and stir in apples. Place in the refrigerator. Let sit for 2–24 hours. Add champagne/sparkling wine, stir and serve. Serves 4–6.

*As made on BookGirlTV video interview with Helen Wan.

ALSO RECOMMENDED:
Confessions of a Minority Darling by Helen Wan (for *The Daily Beast*): A striking article on the complex reality that minorities face in today's society.   http://www.thedailybeast.com/witw/articles/2013/09/17/julie-chen-ethnicity-in-the-workplace-and-confessions-of-a-minority-darling.html

VIRGINIA WOOLF

Between the Acts

A deline Virginia Stephen, born in London in 1882, was bi-polar. She never attended school, but instead largely educated herself by reading in her father's extensive library. In 1912 she married Leonard Woolf, who provided her with the stability she needed to write. Together they founded the Hogarth Press and published work by T. S. Eliot and Katherine Mansfield, among others. A prolific writer of exquisite prose, Virginia wrote six volumes of diaries, six volumes of letters, and many essays. Three of her novels, *Mrs. Dalloway* (1925), *To the Lighthouse* (1927), and *The Waves* (1931) constitute her claim to fame as a modernist writer.

In 1941, Virginia Woolf drowned herself in the River Ouse, near Rodmell in Sussex, by putting rocks in her coat pockets. Her suicide note read:

"Dearest, I feel certain I am going mad again...And I shan't recover this time...I am doing what seems the best thing to do...I can't fight any longer...Everything has gone from me but the certainty of your goodness. I can't go on spoiling your life any longer...I don't think two people could have been happier than we have been. V."

Before she died, she was working on a manuscript called *Between the Acts* in which, it seems, she might have been rehearsing her own demise.

From *Between the Acts*:
"A grain fell and spiraled down; a petal fell, filled and sank. At that the fleet of boat-shaped bodies paused; poised; equipped; mailed; then with a waver of undulation off they flashed. It was in that deep centre, in that black heart, that the lady had drowned herself."

FITZROY FIZZ

Virginia Woolf lived at 29 Fitzroy Square, which is marked with a blue plaque, from 1907–1911. The square, named after Charles Fitzroy, fourth Duke of Grafton, dates back to 1794, and was a film location for the 2009 BBC adaptation of Jane Austen's *Emma*.

Stone's Original Ginger Wine

Champagne

Pour Stone's Original Ginger Wine into chilled flute glass. Top with champagne.

ALSO RECOMMENDED:
Orlando: A Biography. An influential, semi-biographical novel published in 1928, considered one of Woolf's most accessible novels.

DAN ZEVIN

Dan Gets a Minivan

Dan Zevin grew up in suburban New Jersey, the son of a gynecologist father and a mother whom he credits with imbuing him with humor. In school, Dan's lone academic skill was in writing book reports. His passion was *Rolling Stone*, which led to an internship there while he majored in journalism at New York University. Zevin moved on to teaching journalism classes and writing about the finer points of athletic equipment for a men's health magazine. On assignment to review fitness-walking videos, he instead submitted a parody review to *Spy*, the satirical magazine of late-1980s New York. When it was published, Zevin committed to writing humor.

After college he moved to Boston with his girlfriend (now wife), Megan Tingley. He became a humor columnist for Boston-area newspapers and wrote for *Details* and *Maxim*. Through his former editor at *Rolling Stone*, Zevin sent the manuscript for his first book to an agent, who gave it to another agent, who became his agent.

Beginning with *Entry-Level Life* (1998), Zevin has written four books that trace his transition from post-college blues to functional working adult to enthusiastic Costco shopper.

In his 2013 memoir *Dan Gets a Minivan*, Zevin chronicles his evolution from free-and-easy career guy to stay-at-home father. In addition to his books, Zevin has taught humor writing at Sarah Lawrence College and Fordham University, and is a popular comic correspondent for NPR. In 2013, he won the Thurber Prize for Humor.

From *Dan Gets a Minivan*:
"Most men drift through life in a fog, waiting for some moment of clarity to give them purpose and meaning. I should know; I used to be one of them. But then something changed."

KIR ROYALE CHAMPAGNE COCKTAIL

On date night, the author and his wife drink champagne cocktails in an intimate French restaurant they used to frequent before having kids, and reflect on the only thing they really need after so many years of marriage: a flat screen TV.

- **1 part crème de cassis**
- **5 parts Champagne**
- **1 maraschino cherry**

Pour crème de cassis into a glass and gently pour champagne on top. Garnish with cherry. Serves 1.

ALSO RECOMMENDED:

The Day I Turned Uncool: Confessions of a Reluctant Grown-Up. Comic tales about Dan's experiences, such as a disturbing new interest in lawn care, as he moves from his twenties to his thirties.

ACKNOWLEDGMENTS

Love and thanks to my family for their unfailing support: my husband Dan, my kids Danni and Phillip, and my mum, Barbara. I love you all very much. Also, heartfelt thanks to Cynthia Manson, Kitty Florey, David Klein, Stephanie Bowen, and finally, many, many thanks to Leslie Paparo for her invaluable contributions, her friendship, and all the fun!

ABOUT THE AUTHOR

Tessa Smith McGovern is an award-winning short story writer whose many publication credits include the *Connecticut Review* and the English Arts Council at the Southbank Centre, London.

As a child growing up in Surrey, England, she loved to read. Her favorite book was a large, gloriously illustrated copy of *The Arabian Nights: Tales from a Thousand and One Nights* in which Scheherazade saved her own life, night after night, by telling stories. Tessa's mother was also an avid reader, and would read beautiful sentences aloud with relish. At the age of ten, during Tessa's parents' acrimonious divorce, she began to keep a journal and, at eleven, was sent to board at an all-girls Church of England convent school. At sixteen, she left school, worked an assortment of jobs, then set off on her own across Europe, working first in Austria and later in Spain.

She is the founder and editor of eChook Digital Publishing, publisher of short story and memoir collections on multiple platforms: iPhone, iPad, iPod Touch, GooglePlay, Nook, and Kindle, as well as original Web-based stories at echook.com. eChook.com has been visited by thousands of readers in over one hundred countries.

In 2012, eChook Digital Publishing's *Memoir, Vol. 1*, won a silver medal in the eLit Awards and Tessa Smith McGovern's *London Road: Linked* Stories won a gold medal in the eLit Awards.

Tessa is host and executive producer of BookGirlTV, an award-winning web series for readers, writers, and book clubs featuring book reviews, interviews, and cocktail fun with emerging and bestselling authors. Recent guests include bestselling author Jane

Green, memoirist Dani Shapiro, and feminist and crime author Linda Fairstein.

Tessa lives in Connecticut with her husband, has two children, aged seventeen and twenty-one, and teaches at the Writing Institute at Sarah Lawrence College, Bronxville, New York.

BIBLIOGRAPHY

Allende, Isabel. *Eva Luna*. New York: Random House, LLC, 1987.

Athill, Diana. *Somewhere Towards the End*. New York: W.W. Norton & Company, 2008.

Austen, Jane. *Pride and Prejudice*. New York: Dover Publications, 1995.

Bennett, Alan. *The Complete Talking Heads*. New York: Picador, 1998.

Brontë, Anne. *Agnes Grey*. New York: Alfred A. Knopf, 2012.

Brontë, Charlotte. *Jane Eyre*. New York: Bantam Books, 1981.

Brontë, Emily. *Wuthering Heights*. London: Puffin Books, 1990.

Cather, Willa. *Cather Novels & Stories 1905–1918*. New York, Library of America, 1987.

Chopin, Kate. *The Awakening*. New York: The Library of America, 2002.

Collette. *Chéri*. Mineola: Dover Publications, 2001.

Díaz, Junot. *This Is How You Lose Her*. New York: Penguin Group, LLC, 2012.

Dickens, Charles. *David Copperfield*. Mineola: Dover Publications, 2005.

Dunbar, Olivia Howard. *The Shell of Sense*. Uncasville: Richard H. Fawcett Publisher, 1997.

Faulkner, William. *As I Lay Dying*. New York: Random House, 1958.

Fitzgerald, F. Scott. *The Great Gatsby*. New York: Scribner Publishing, 1925.

Gaskell, Elizabeth. *Mary Barton*. New York: Penguin Books, 1996

Gilman, Charlotte Perkins. *The Yellow Wall-Paper, Herland, and Selected Writings*. New York: Penguin Classics, 2009.

Godwin, Gail. *Evenings at Five*. New York: Random House, 2003.

Green, Jane. *Another Piece of My Heart*. New York: St. Martin's Press, 2012.

Hansberry, Lorraine. *To Be Young, Gifted and Black: Lorraine Hansberry In Her Own Words*. New York: Simon & Schuster Publishing Group, 1969.

Hemingway, Ernest. *The Old Man and the Sea*. New York: Scribner Publishing Group, 1952.

Heyer, Georgette. *Friday's Child*. Naperville: Sourcebooks, 2008.

Hurston, Zora Neale. *The Complete Stories*. New York: HarperCollins Publishers, 1995.

Joyce, James. *Ulysses*. Based on the pre-1923 print editions, Project Gutenberg, 2003. http://www.gutenberg.org/ebooks/4300.

Kincaid, Jamaica. *The Autobiography of My Mother*. New York: Farrar, Straus and Giroux, LLC,1996.

Lahiri, Jhumpa. *The Namesake*. New York: Houghton Mifflin Harcourt Publishing, 2003.

Lamb, Wally. *I Know This Much Is True*. New York: HarperCollins Publishers, 1998.

Lester, Joan Steinau. *Mama's Child*. New York: Atria Publishing Group, 2013.

Lurie, Alison. *The Last Resort*. New York: Random House, 1998.

Mansfield, Katherine. *The Collected Stories of Katherine Mansfield*. London: Wordsworth Classics, 2006.

Munro, Alice. *Runaway*. New York: Alfred A. Knopf, 2004.

O'Connor, Flannery. *A Good Man is Hard to Find and Other Stories*. New York: Houghton Mifflin Harcourt Publishing Company, 1953.

Oates, Joyce Carol. *After the Wreck, I Picked Myself Up, Spread My Wings, and Flew Away*. New York: HarperCollins Publishers, 2006.

Parker, Dorothy. *The Portable Dorothy Parker*. New York: Penguin Group, LLC, 1928.

Porter, Katherine Anne. *Pale Horse, Pale Rider: Three Short Novels*. New York: Houghton Mifflin Harcourt Publishing Company, 1937.

Quick, Matthew. *The Silver Linings Playbook*. New York: Farrar, Straus and Giroux, LLC, 2008.

Sankovitch, Nina. *Tolstoy and the Purple Chair*. New York: HarperCollins Publishers, 2011.

Shapiro, Dani. *Devotion*. New York: HarperCollins Publishers, 2010.

Shelley, Mary. *Frankenstein*. New York: Barnes and Noble Classics, 2003.

Shelton, Sandi Kahn. *Kissing Games of the World: A Novel*. New York: Random House Publishing, 2008.

Taylor, Elizabeth. *The Complete Short Stories*. London: Virago Press, 2012.

Thompson, Christina. *Come on Shore and We Will Kill and Eat You All*. New York: Bloomsbury Publishing, 2008.

Trevor, William. *My House in Umbria*. New York: Penguin Group, LLC, 1991.

Trollope, Joanna. *Other People's Children*. New York: Penguin Group, LLC, 1998.

Tsukiyama, Gail. *Women of the Silk*. New York: St. Martin's Press, 1991.

Tyler, Anne. *Saint Maybe*. New York: Random House LLC, 1991.

Umrigar, Thrity. *First Darling of the Morning*. New York: HarperCollins Publishers, 2008.

Wan, Helen. *The Partner Track*. New York: St. Martin's Press, 2013.

Woolf, Virginia. *Between the Acts*. New York: Houghton Mifflin Harcourt Publishing Company, 1941.

Zevin, Dan. *Dan Gets a Minivan: Life at the Intersection of Dude and Dad*. New York: Scribner Publishing, 2012.

TEXT PERMISSIONS

Lahiri. © 2003 by Jhumpa Lahiri. Reprinted by permission of Houghton Mifflin Harcourt Publishing Company. All rights reserved.

Wally Lamb—Brief excerpt from p. 47 from I KNOW THIS MUCH IS TRUE by Wally Lamb. © 1998 by Wally Lamb. Reprinted by permission of HarperCollins Publishers.

Joan Steinau Lester—Reprinted with the permission of Atria Publishing Group from MAMA'S CHILD by Joan Steinau Lester. © 2013 by Joan Steinau Lester. All rights reserved.

Alison Lurie—© 1998 by Alison Lurie.

Katherine Mansfield—PD.

Alice Munro—Excerpt from RUNAWAY: STORIES by Alice Munro. © 2004 by Alice Munro. Used by permission of Alfred A. Knopf, an imprint of the Knopf Doubleday Publishing Group, a division of Random House LLC. All rights reserved.

Joyce Carol Oates—Used by permission of HarperCollins Publishers.

Flannery O'Connor—Excerpt from "Good Country People" from A GOOD MAN IS HARD TO FIND AND OTHER STORIES by Flannery O'Connor. © 1955 by Flannery O'Connor. © renewed 1983 by Flannery O'Connor. Used by permission of Houghton Mifflin Harcourt Publishing Company. All rights reserved.

Dorothy Parker—Excerpt from "The Custard Heart" © 1928, renewed © 1956 by Dorothy Parker. From THE PORTABLE DOROTHY PARKER by Dorothy Parker, edited by Marion Meade. Used by permission of Viking Penguin, a division of Penguin Group (USA) LLC.

Katherine Anne Porter—Excerpt from "Pale Horse, Pale Rider" from PALE HORSE, PALE RIDER: THREE SHORT NOVELS by Katherine Anne Porter. © 1937 by Katherine Anne Porter. © renewed 1965 by Katherine Anne Porter. Used by permission of Houghton Mifflin Harcourt Publishing Company. All rights reserved.

Matthew Quick—Excerpt from "An Infinite amount of Days Until My Inevitable Reunion with Nikki" from THE SILVER

PHOTO CREDITS

INDEX

C

M

N

O

S